NATURAL FITNESS

Bruce Tulloh

Illustrations by
CAROL MONGO

SIMON AND SCHUSTER · NEW YORK

PUBLISHED BY SIMON AND SCHUSTER
A DIVISION OF GULF & WESTERN CORPORATION
SIMON & SCHUSTER BUILDING
ROCKEFELLER CENTER
1230 AVENUE OF THE AMERICAS
NEW YORK, NEW YORK 10020

DESIGNED BY EVE METZ
MANUFACTURED IN THE UNITED STATES OF AMERICA

1 2 3 4 5 6 7 8 9 10

LIBRARY OF CONGRESS CATALOGING IN PUBLICATION DATA

TULLOH, BRUCE.
    NATURAL FITNESS.
    BRITISH ED. PUBLISHED IN 1976 UNDER TITLE:
NATURALLY FIT.
    BIBLIOGRAPHY: P.
    INCLUDES INDEX.
    1. EXERCISE. 2. PHYSICAL FITNESS. I. TITLE.
RA781.T84   1977   613.7′1   77–2166

ISBN 0–671–22615–0

CONTENTS

5

INTRODUCTION

This book is not for athletes or doctors, nor is it for biologists or coaches. Most of them know how to live, and if they fail to follow their own advice they have only themselves to blame. This book is for the man or woman who wants to find the best way to live. The greater part of it is common scientific knowledge and a small part is based on my own observation and experience. Trying to keep it simple and avoid scientific jargon, I may at times have explained things that are already understood, but I want to make sure that the message is clear.

We spend a lot of time and money on maintaining and improving our houses and our cars. That makes sense, because we want to get the best out of them and make them last as long as possible. I want you to take yourself just as seriously, to think about what you eat and what you do, so that you can get the most out of life. Your body is your most valuable asset, but if you do nothing until you are ill, it is too late—the machine has already started to go wrong. The earlier in your life you can start living the right way, the less time you will spend at the doctor's. More important still, if you are healthy you can lead a full, happy and useful life. In this book you will find some guidelines; the rest is up to you.

1

The Natural Life: Man the Hunter

Out on the plains, in a hot, dry land, a small line of hunters moves through the bush. They are spread out in a crescent, three on either side of the leader, with about twenty paces between each man and the next. They advance silently, on bare feet, moving upwind toward a herd of grazing waterbuck. The leader is watching the sentries on the edge of the herd, alert to any change in their behavior. The men pause, then move on again. When they are seventy paces from the herd, a buck throws up its head and starts to move. At that moment the men charge in, yelling, waving spears, kicking up dust. The animals stampede, the line of flight taking them toward an escarpment of rock. Turned by the escarpment and chased by the hunters, the herd is forced toward a narrow defile and the ambush that awaits them. The spears fly out from the waiting men, heavy buck go down in a cloud of dust and the two parties of hunters go in with clubs and stabbing swords to finish off the wounded animals.

Before the sun goes down the hunting party, bellies full of fresh meat, is back at the camp with skins and carcasses for wives and children. The day ends with feasting, dancing, stories and laughter; the fires die down and the hunters lie down with their families and sleep until the next dawn.

9

That was the way it was for a very long time. Our human ancestors were undoubtedly hunting animals, though they did not live by that alone. All the evidence that has been collected points to a life that relied on gathering as well as hunting. Evidence comes from the animal remains found associated with the human bones, from the tools associated with them and from the actual skulls. From the bones and cave drawings we know that primitive man was a meat eater, but we also know that his diet included a wide variety of fruits, seeds, roots and other plant material. Not only have vegetable fragments been found in the "garbage dumps" of cave dwellings, but also the structure of human teeth tells us without a doubt that man is an omnivore. Like pigs and rats, we can cope with either vegetable or animal food; our teeth are suited both for slicing and for crushing and grinding.

In spite of this evidence, there are a lot of people who will produce lengthy arguments which claim to show that man should be a vegetarian. But how do they explain the fact that the human stomach produces pepsin, an enzyme that digests animal protein? Or the fact that human cells are unable to manufacture certain amino acids which are needed for continued growth? All these amino acids are present in meat, but no single vegetable food contains them all. If further evidence is needed, we must look at the hunting-gathering tribes that still remain in the world. Now forming only a very small fraction of the earth's population, they have been driven by the shepherds and farmers to the fringes of the habitable world, the land on which no one else will live. Even so, none of these tribes is either exclusively vegetarian or exclusively carnivorous.

In recent years anthropologists have made close studies of the remaining hunting-and-gathering tribes. These studies are important to us, because they show humans close to their original state—ourselves as we once were. It is like being in a time machine and going back a hundred thousand years.

Since these peoples have been pushed out of the good hunting land onto the margins of existence, it is hard to say exactly which is most typical of the natural man, but we can be fairly sure that the traits they have in common are also traits we once shared. Those tribes living in the jungles of the Congo, the Amazon and Southeast Asia will obviously differ greatly from the remaining North American Indians who live on the edge of the cold lands, and both will differ from the bushmen of southern and eastern Africa and Australia. Even so, there are common features.

First of all, the size of the tribe is fairly constant: about five hundred people, including children, living in family groups. Most tribes are seminomadic, moving according to the seasons. In the semidesert regions the tribe is confined to the region of the water-holes during the dry season, traveling farther afield after the rains. In the case of the Kung bushmen, living on the edge of the Kalahari desert, the tribe can find all its food within a six-mile radius of the camp. Contrary to what most people think, the life of such a people is not hard.

In a three-week study it was found that the Kung bushmen hunted or gathered food an average of two and a half days a week, the working day itself being only about six hours long. The nine-to-five commuting citizen may well reflect on whether civilization has been entirely a good thing! Nor was their diet a poor one. Their protein intake was well above the recommended daily minimum of the Food and Agriculture Organization. Their caloric intake was over 2,100 calories per day—less than that needed in a temperate climate, but perfectly adequate for someone living in a hot climate, where little energy is needed to keep the body warm. What was particularly impressive was the range of their diet. About one-third of the total food was provided by the men, hunting for meat; the rest was provided by the women and children, collecting vegetable foods. In this dry and apparently inhospitable land the tribe used more than eighty different kinds of plants for food, but being careful not to exhaust their food reserves, they used most of these plants very infrequently. In view of this varied and balanced diet, it is not surprising that the tribe does not suffer from any of the deficiency diseases that we almost automatically expect to find in "underdeveloped" countries.

This pattern of food collection from a wide range is repeated in most of the other tribes that have been studied. The Hadza of Tanzania get about one-fifth of their food supply in meat and the rest from vegetable sources and in the form of wild honey. The hunter-gatherers on the southern edge of the Sahara eat fish, reptiles, birds, mushrooms, water lily roots, succulent leaves, nuts, wild grains, shellfish and locusts as well as meat from gazelles and hyraxes. In the forest tribes the range of available food is far wider and continuous throughout the year. Among the bushmen of the Ituri, like the Hadza and the Kung, diseases such as kwashiorkor, rickets, scurvy and vitamin-B deficiency do not occur.

Of course, one finds exceptions to this pattern of a balanced diet in the tribes living at the colder extremes of climate. The farther north you go, the smaller is the proportion of vegetable foods in the diet. On the northwest coast of America there are still Indian and Eskimo tribes living in the traditional hunting way. Tribes such as the Kwakiutl, the Eyak and the Chinook get twenty to thirty percent of their food from vegetable sources, the Ingalik and the Nunamiut only ten percent, and the Chipewyan and the Nootka virtually none at all. In the traditional diet of the Nootka, before any foods were imported, the only sugar was provided by a few berries in the summer, while all the starch they had was from roots, available only when the ground was unfrozen. The diet of these tribes was therefore very high in protein, fats and oils, all from animal sources.

I have mentioned these exceptions because they do show how adaptable an animal the human is; but we should not allow that to obscure the main point of the argument, which is that in the natural state the human had a very wide-ranging diet, obtained mainly from vegetable sources but with meat forming between one-quarter and one-third. One more point should be mentioned. The diet was not always a regular one—at least, not regular in our "three meals a day" fashion. Although plant food would always be available, meat was eaten mainly on the day of a kill or the day after; this might mean four large meat meals a week in a good week and only one in a poor week.

What sort of health did these people enjoy? From the living

evidence, pretty good. In the study of the Kung, ten percent of the population were found to be over the age of sixty. When one considers that the life expectancy in the poorer agricultural countries is often under forty years, and that the same was true in many Western industrialized countries in the nineteenth century, it says a lot for the primitive life. The general health of our primitive ancestors was good, thanks to good nutrition and plenty of exercise; it may also have owed something to the lack of additives in their diet—by which I do not mean artificial flavorings or preservatives: I mean salt and sugar. There is good evidence for the belief that excess salt leads to increase in blood pressure and also for the belief that increase in weight leads to increase in blood pressure. The high blood pressure in turn leads to increased risk of strokes, heart ailments and kidney disease.

What is impressive about the Kung is the fact that they do not suffer from increasing blood pressure with increasing age. In the fifteen-to-nineteen age group the mean blood pressures were 117/73*—a normal figure, with none outside the normal range; in the forty-to-forty-nine age group the means were almost exactly the same—116/74; in the seventy-to-eighty age group the pressure means were 120/67. A series of readings taken on an Amazonian forest tribe showed the same pattern as that of the African bushmen—no rise with age. By comparison, A National Health Survey in the United States has shown that fifteen percent of the population between ages eighteen and forty-nine have pressures exceeding 140/90, and at ages fifty-five and over this proportion rises to twenty-five percent. Currently, at least twenty-three million Americans are believed to be definitely hypertensive, with blood pressures of 160/95 or greater.

As well as the steady blood pressure, which may possibly have a connection with the low salt content of their diet, one finds that the Kung bushmen have very little obesity. Their body weight is

---

* Blood-pressure measurements are given in terms of millimeters of mercury. The first figure refers to the systolic pressure, which is the pressure with which the heart pumps blood into the arteries, and the second to the diastolic pressure, which is the pressure between beats.

low, even for their small size, but these may both be specializations to suit their hot-climate life. We can assume that the Cro-Magnon ancestors of European man were similar in size to the present-day inhabitants—their skeletons seem to support this view. However, one would expect that the colder countries would favor the selection of a slightly larger variety of human, because the heat loss is proportionately less from the large man than from the small. Larger people would have a proportionately higher caloric intake.

What we can say is that although the actual food intake varied with the climate, the natural man was very rarely fat. It was in the very nature of his life that getting food required exercise. If a man became fat he would move too slowly and heat up too much to be an efficient hunter. The fat man is a symbol of the surplus society. This implies, though we cannot be completely certain, that the natural man did not suffer from the degenerative diseases—the diseases of old age that catch up with civilized man, such as heart attacks, strokes, diabetes and emphysema. About cancer we cannot be sure, though obviously the incidence of lung cancer would be lower in primitive societies—unless a family lived in a particularly smoky cave!

This may all sound too good to be true. Why, then, did all these people not live to be eighty years old? The answer is that they were vulnerable in several ways. First, there was probably a high incidence of internal parasites. This applies particularly to the forest dwellers. Among living hunter-gatherers it was found that members of one group of African bushmen had on average three types of parasites each: two types of fluke or tapeworm and one type of blood protozoan (the malarial and the sleeping-sickness parasites are of this kind). In jungle dwellers in Malaysia the parasite count was twenty-two types per man, and in a Pygmy tribe, living in a rain forest in central Africa, it was twenty types. These include tapeworms and other parasites in the intestines, hookworms and threadworms, whose combined effect is to divert food from the human host to the parasite, thus weakening the host and, at the least, shortening his life-span. In some cases the parasite will kill

14

him in a few weeks, in others weaken him so that he cannot hunt but wastes away over a period of a few years.

The second disadvantage was the risk of infection by bacteria and viruses. Although, like many wild animals, primitive man probably developed resistance to many common infective organisms, a new strain of, say, influenza or cholera could cause disaster. Extreme examples have been seen in cases where Europeans have brought new strains of microorganisms into previously stable populations—for instance in South America, where the Inca civilization of Peru was destroyed by the Spanish diseases rather than by the Spanish themselves, and in the South Sea Islands. In the same way disease could suddenly ravage an isolated tribe that had no natural resistance. Infection of wounds, too, is a cause of death that arises far more frequently among hunting tribes than among farmers. With no antibiotics or disinfectants available, a simple cut or a bite could prove fatal.

The third area of vulnerability was simply accidents, in which we must also include such occurrences as the burst appendix, failure of the food supply and death in childbirth, of both mother and child. In a community where life was active and where prestige depended on success in hunting, it was inevitable that risks would be taken. This would lead to two peak periods of accidents —among adolescents, trying to prove their ability, and among the older warriors, trying to preserve their domination when their strength and speed of movement were starting to fail. When a man spends all his life competing for survival with large carnivores, coexisting with snakes and scorpions and competing for territory with neighboring tribes, he needs to have everything going for him—luck, skill, experience and the support of his friends; should any of these fail him, he will not survive.

During most of his life on earth, man has been part of the ecosystem, expanding as far as the food supply will allow, but in competition with other large mammals. The tribe could not increase too much in size, for if it did there would be an inadequate food supply, or else infringement of somebody else's hunting grounds. The first would lead to a drop in the number of children surviving, because of the effect of malnutrition on the mothers; the second would cause an even more direct drop in the population as the tribes went to war. Over the course of time the typical hunter-gatherer community, therefore, reached a relatively stable population limit in which the natural tendency to increase in numbers was held in check by the adult death rate, the infantile death rate and whatever form of birth control was practiced. There is evidence that birth control, abortion and infanticide by exposure were used in many tribes.

Leaving aside health and diet, what kind of people were they? What was the pattern of their emotional life? As I shall explain later, the basic drives of the personality owe a lot to evolutionary background. The inbuilt needs, instincts and aggressions of the natural man and woman, fitted to the demands of a million years, have survived through the herding and the farming stages into our industrial society; the character of the hunter-gatherer is to a large extent our character.

It is common to think of the life of primitive man as a constant savage struggle against his environment. This is because we ourselves, sitting in centrally heated and air-conditioned houses and collecting our food from the supermarket, can imagine nothing more dreadful than having to get up at dawn and hunt our food with a spear or a bow. However, to the man born and bred in the open, that life would appear entirely normal. In studying existing tribes we find that they lead leisured lives, spending only a few hours each week in hunting. They have no deep-rooted anxieties about the future, demonstrated by the fact that they do not store more than a few days' supply of food. The hunting is a vital part of life, but it is not the whole of life.

In his natural habitat primitive man was like Br'er Rabbit in the briar patch. His food supplies were known from an early age— some plentiful but unexciting; some uncommon but delicious, like wild honey; some to be eaten only in hard times. The dangers were there, certainly, but they were familiar dangers. The danger of going out hunting when lions were on the move was rather like running across a busy street in the rush hour—you were taking a chance by doing it, and if you got into trouble it was your own fault. The education of the child was in learning the customs of the tribe. In the tribal experience lay all the answers to the situations that might be met, but they were not so much formulated as a set of rules as embodied in the legends that were passed down through the tribe, the stories that were told around the fires.

Being completely at home in his surroundings, primitive man was not an anxious creature, but he was prepared for the challenges that he had to face. This can be seen in the daily life of the Ainu, which has been studied by Japanese anthropologists. This people, thought to be the aboriginal inhabitants of the Japanese islands, live in the northern areas, where some still continue to live in the traditional way. Since their climate is temperate rather than tropical, their life is governed by the seasons far more than that of the desert or forest dwellers. They live in the river valleys, where they have permanent settlements, in spring fishing the rivers and hunting bears in the mountainous region at the heads of the rivers. As summer approaches they change to collecting the plentiful plants in the valleys, and they also grow some crops and continue to fish and hunt. In the autumn, as the plant supply diminishes, the men move up to their hunting huts in the mountains, where they hunt deer for both meat and skins. When the snow comes they return to their settlements, to their main winter occupation of trapping and bear hunting, as well as the collection of any available plant material—roots, bark and buds.

For the hunter-gatherers in a very cold climate, life is certainly harder. More work and more preparation must be done in the autumn if the tribe is to survive through the winter. However, generations of this kind of life will eventually have adapted these people to it biologically. Their diet will be different from that of the tropical peoples, because very little vegetable food is available in winter. The need to hunt in cold weather will encourage the development of bigger and stronger men, with more fat for insulation, more muscle for fighting the large mammals and more endurance for going without food while hunting in winter. These differences, however, will not be very clear-cut, although we see extreme examples in the Eskimo on the one hand and the Pygmies of the tropical forest on the other, because the fluctuations in the earth's climate have been considerable during the time since man evolved.

One important but often unrecognized adaptation to the hunting life, one that still remains with us, is the working of the body's hormonal mechanisms. Everybody knows that we produce adrenaline—the hormone of "fight or flight"—when we find ourselves in an exciting or dangerous situation. This prepares our body for the emergencies of fighting or running away, by accelerating the heartbeat and the rate of breathing. In the same way the body prepares itself for peaks of activity in spring and autumn under the influence of an "internal clock." Endocrinologists, whose field is the study of hormone systems, have discovered that the whole series of circadian rhythms—which operate on a twenty-four-hour cycle, making you more alert at certain times of the day and more lethargic at other times—is governed by hormonal secretions. That after-lunch lethargy that always overtakes me in the middle of the day is not so much the result of overeating as the result of evolution. In the middle of the day, hunting stops. The carnivores hunt in the morning and the evening, but not at noon, and the activities of the human hunter too are diminished at this time.

As well as the daily rhythm and the yearly rhythm, there are the variations over monthly and weekly periods. And perhaps most important of all is the "clockwork" that controls our physical and emotional development over our whole life-span. It is no good trying to live the same kind of life at forty as you did at eighteen when your hormonal makeup has changed. Because your body is different, you no longer give the same responses to particular stimuli.

The body of primitive man was programmed by the force of evolution, over hundreds of thousands of years, to give the necessary responses to the challenges of his life. First, evolution favors the animal with the faster breeding rate. Man therefore developed a strong mating instinct. Second, he had to survive in competition with animals that were stronger, faster and better equipped for hunting than he was. He therefore developed his greatest weapons, his hands and his brain, so that by the use of weapons and social cooperation he became the dominant species. Third, he had to survive in competition with other men and probably with other species of men or ape-men who coexisted with him. This led to the aggressive territory-defending instincts so prized in the modern business world.

Depending on the environment, the selection pressure would at times favor the socially cooperative aspect of human nature and at times the competitive aspect. The logical and most effective blend of these two contradictory instincts appears in the nature of the "tribal man." Here we have cooperation within the tribes and competition between them. Unless its food supply is unlimited, this tribal organization is a tremendous advantage to the species that has it and is found in the monkeys, the baboons and some of the anthropoid apes. It must have been part of human society from the very earliest times, remaining built into our genetic makeup just as securely as the genes that condition the shape of our hands and our teeth.

Man is a tribal animal and this must be taken into account in considering the way in which we should live, as I shall do in a later chapter. We know that the life of the tribe was built around hunting, food gathering, having children and defending territory. Was there anything else? There certainly was. I have already stated that the life of the Paleolithic hunter was not desperately hard. Although it must have been harder for the tribes in colder climates, there was still a lot of time left for leisure. Remember that the hunters of the Kung bushmen worked only a fifteen-hour week? With an intelligent brain, primitive man did not spend all his spare time asleep—he worked out a comprehensive culture system that brought together the material and emotional needs of every member of the tribe and gave them significance. The rituals, the magic, the games, the sacrifices that developed in the different tribes all filled particular needs. If they had not, they would not have survived.

19

NATURAL FITNESS

Let us try to consider what these needs might be, sticking as closely as possible to the traits that members of the tribe needed to make them effective. These traits, which were important to them, will also be important to us, because we have the same temperamental makeup.

The cultural system must offer instruction to the young and an opportunity to develop strength and skill. For the young of both sexes it must offer initiation or enrollment into adult society, so that they have the confidence to fill the roles for which they are equipped. For the adult hunter it must offer control, or at least a sense of control, over his environment, so that he can hunt as effectively as possible. For the adult female it must offer internal stability, so that she can bring up her children without domestic stress. For the old it must offer the status that will give them the authority to use their wisdom for the good of the tribe.

Consider a moment the role of the old men and women. They must have had a use. Why is it that humans can live for seventy or eighty years whereas other hunting mammals live to a maximum of fifteen or twenty? The answer is that man's success has been due to his ability to control his environment, and this ability lies in the accumulation of experience. Patterns of climate, movement of herds of game and carnivores, incidence of pests and diseases repeat themselves only over very long cycles, running into tens of years. Only in the case of an animal that can talk is extreme longevity an advantage. Thus the old man with firsthand experience of all the incidents that might befall the tribe was of great value even if he had not the strength to hunt for his own food. In a world of uncertainty and threats, the wisdom of the tribe, embodied in the elders, provided certainty.

Lastly, the cultural system must offer rewards to all its members for their efforts. The incentives must make them happy, adjust them to their role in life and, perhaps most important of all, bind them together as a tribe.

In the primitive tribe, the tribal religion served every emotional need. Every biological drive that was not worked out in the fighting and hunting was provided for in the dancing, the feasting, the magic and the dreams that formed part of the life. For every occasion there was a precedent, a ritual, a piece of magic to propitiate the gods. There was no distinction between what was work, what was leisure and what was religion, because all were part of a unified whole, and the whole system was itself part of the surroundings. As the seasons changed, so did the magic. As you grew older, so your role in the ritual changed. As long as you performed the proper rituals, you knew that you were doing all that you could.

Was primitive man different from us? In the face of tremendous uncertainties, he banded together with his fellows for reassurance. He could work very hard at times, but he also spent a lot of time lazing about. He could show great courage in a battle or a hunt, but after that he liked to relax with eating, drinking and telling tales of his bravery. He enjoyed the releasing effect of alcohol and other drugs, and he enjoyed sex.

If there is a difference, it is only in the structure of his society. The life of primitive man, like that of any other animal, was fundamentally stable. The seasons turned, men were born and men died, but the life of the tribe, the size of the tribe and the wealth of the tribe remained the same, in tune with its surroundings, over tens of thousands of years. There is a lesson to be drawn from this and I shall return to it later.

2

The Natural Life: Man the Farmer

In the Rift Valley of Kenya the cattle herds of the Masai move from one scanty grazing ground to another, followed by the tribal unit, a group of related families. Life is lived entirely out in the open, with no permanent home, only temporary shelters—manvattas—used for sleeping and no possessions that cannot walk or be carried. The Masai have taken one aspect of the primitive life and have developed it to its ultimate. Whereas the primitive hunter followed the migrating game herds, the pastoral nomad has controlled the animals and made himself independent of the wild. It is a way of life that has obvious advantages over hunting and gathering. It has been estimated that the hunter needed almost four square miles of land to get enough food for his family; the herdsman can maintain enough cattle for one family on much less than one square kilometer of good grazing.

The Masai obtain most of their needs from the cattle—as the Plains Indians did from the bison: meat, milk, blood, hides and dung. In the warm and mainly dry climate of East Africa neither shelter nor clothing need be elaborate, and the only foreign material employed in the traditional Masai life is the metal in the spears. Indeed, until the twentieth century flint was still being used alongside steel; I have been to places where half-made arrowheads still lie on the bare soil. The Masai, a large tribe spread over thousands of square miles of Kenya and Tanzania, have so far, in common with many other tribes, felt little need to alter their way of life in spite of a hundred years of contact with European culture. Provided that they have the space to graze their cattle, life is pretty good: there is very little work and a great deal of freedom, because their demands are not great, and there is consequently a lot of time for the traditional Masai pastimes— fighting, cattle raiding, drinking, philosophizing and asking rather sophisticated riddles.

The general health of the nomads is surprisingly good considering the nature of their diet. Having "specialized" by taking up the pastoral life, they have also restricted themselves to a diet mostly of blood, meat and milk. A study of the Samburu, a similar East African nomadic tribe, found that some men drank up to ten quarts of milk a day and that five or six quarts was quite normal. The older men drank less milk but ate more meat. Apart from a little corn, no vegetable food was eaten at all. Although these nomads do get some carbohydrate from corn, their diet is far, far, higher in animal products than the balanced diet of the hunter-gatherer.

This kind of diet would be considered extremely risky by most American doctors because of the high cholesterol intake, which has been associated with hardening of the arteries, high blood pressure and heart diseases. But in Africa, no such thing occurs. In the group of Samburu who were studied, which included elders up to ninety years old, there was no increase in body weight with age and practically no increase in blood pressure with age, as can be seen from Table 1 (p. 24).

The workers on this particular study, like many others dealing with pastoral and hunting communities, found no evidence of gross cardiovascular disease. Quite clearly, the cholesterol alone does not cause the troubles of the civilized man.

There are three main ways in which the Samburu differ from the average European or American: their diet contains very little carbohydrate, their bodies are very much the long and thin (ectomorphic) type and they take a great deal of exercise. On a strictly scientific basis, any of those factors could be the secret of their cardiovascular fitness, or all three could have a bearing on it.

TABLE 1

Age group	Blood-pressure Means	
	Samburu (male)	U.S. (male)
20–29	111.5/76.5	121.4/74.2
30–39	112.3/76.7	122.9/76.3
40–49	112.2/78.8	125.5/78.2
50–59	109.2/74.9	129.1/79.5
60 and over	116.6/74.8	132.4/79.6

We know that certain physical types are more prone to high blood pressure than others. The ectomorph is generally less likely to develop it than the muscular, stocky type of person. As far as the eating of carbohydrate is concerned, there is always a balance between the number of calories eaten and the number used up. A person who is not eating much carbohydrate is unlikely to have a very high caloric intake, and if he is taking a lot of exercise he is using up a lot of calories. In such a situation the fat molecules that might have gone to form cholesterol will be burned up by the exercise.

The amount of exercise that the human frame can take is perhaps better demonstrated by these nomads than by any other group, because it is part of their way of life. A daily walk-jog of thirty miles—or even forty miles—is not considered inordinate; much more than this may be done occasionally in a single day. A Masai raiding party, composed not of picked athletes, selected and trained for running ability, but of all the men in the warrior age group, may run fifteen or twenty miles in an evening, fight a skirmish and run back again. These are the men who have moved only one step from the primitive life and have retained the natural level of activity for which their bodies were designed.

Although the level of health and fitness among the young nomads is high, the general condition of the tribes is far from ideal. They are just as prone to infectious diseases as the primitive hunter-gatherer tribes, tuberculosis and other chest diseases bringing down the expectancy of life. Parasites are not very common in the dry habitats in which they live, but eye diseases are and are probably spread by the flies that are found with their cattle.

The greatest limiting factor on these people is space, the spread of agriculture restricting the boundaries of their territories. The effects of central government, medical programs and improved cattle breeding have all tended to increase the pressure on the land they occupy. At the same time, the rule of law has, in theory, put an end to what was once a natural process of population control: intertribal warfare. The tribal organization of most of the East African tribes produced a warrior age group, whose role, after a prolonged and dramatic initiation ceremony, was war, cattle raiding and wife stealing. When the competition between neighboring tribes has over the years produced such a warrior cult, it cannot be eliminated by a stroke of the pen. The tribal structure and the happiness of the people will survive only if they can find adequate outlets for their natural drives. For some tribes the killing of wild animals such as the lion, also looked on as the raison d'être of the warrior, has now also been forbidden.

In their specialization toward the warrior/shepherd way of life, the pastoral people have developed along a road that may well prove to have a dead end. There are problems already, in the way that the increasing number of cattle reduces the bush to virtual dust-bowl conditions that will support the few but not the many. When cattle become a form of wealth, to be collected merely for prestige rather than for their use, the fragile balance between the people, the cattle and the land is lost.

It is to be hoped that we shall not see the Masai and the Turkana degenerating to the state of the Plains Indians of America. Here were tribes who knew no other life than hunting and fighting. When they were confined to reservations, their inborn aggression, having no other outlet, exhibited itself in knife fights, wife beating and the driving of fast cars. Since that time their story has been one of degradation, drunkenness and neurosis.

NATURAL FITNESS

What we can learn from these nomads is that it is possible to create a socially satisfactory life, all members of the community sharing common values, without reliance on all the equipment of Western civilization. To return to the Masai, it is usual for those members of the tribe who have been educated, even to university and professional levels, to return to their tribal way of life. Having seen what civilization has to offer, they are prepared to return to their traditions because they feel that the Masai view of what is important in life is also their view. I am not suggesting that Americans and Europeans should take up wearing red cloaks and standing around with spears; but I am pointing out that there is more than one set of values for the conduct of life.

From the health aspect we can learn a lot, too. As we have seen, the nomads show that lifelong fitness can be achieved by the majority of people, that there is no reason for body weight and blood pressure to increase with age and that neither heart disease nor flabby muscles are the inevitable result of age; rather, they depend on the way of life.

The nomadic herdsman, however, represents a divergence from the original pattern, one that has but a limited future. The other way, the way of the settler, has been followed by the majority of humanity. It led first to simple agriculture, which provided a stable supply of food for the hunters; then to medieval subsistence farming, which provided the farmer with most of his needs, and finally to advanced agriculture, which provided a considerable surplus. It was only when farmers could provide a surplus of food that city life could begin to develop.

I suspect that most people regard the life of a farmer as the natural one, but it is not. The agricultural phase of human existence has been only one percent of our total time on earth, and already it is ending. Even so, most of the original hunters developed into agriculturists, and human behavior may have been influenced by the demands made on us during that time, which may be as long as a thousand generations. One can imagine that under the strains of struggling for survival in difficult conditions, certain types of people would be better suited to a farming life. Those who were temperamentally suited would persevere, develop farms and raise families, while the more restless or aggressive went hunting farther afield. It is thus arguable, though impossible to prove, that selection pressure favored those with the temperament of the farmer at the expense of the natural hunter.

We can be fairly certain of our ground in stating that there have been no physical changes in the human during the brief agricultural phase. Anyone who has done much gardening will agree that the human frame is not much suited for digging or weeding. If God or the force of evolution had intended us to be farmers or gardeners, He would have placed our hands nearer the ground and found some way around the backaches that such work brings on! A baboon would make a better gardener than a human being—as far as his skeletal structure is concerned, anyway.

Nevertheless, for economic reasons, the hunter became a farmer. And today we can still find in the world all the stages in this transformation, from the mixed hunter-farmer to the mechanized wheat farmer of Kansas. Has this way of life anything to recommend it? Has it anything to teach us about the way we live?

In domesticating both plants and animals, the farmer has achieved great advantages over the hunter. He has, to a marked degree, controlled his environment to suit his purposes. He has ensured a continuous food supply without the dangers of the hunting life, and by creating a permanent settlement he has given himself the chance to store up wealth. This has tremendous advantages in the temperate climates, because the farmer can store food against the winter, avoiding the uncertainty that was the lot of the hunter. He no longer needs to migrate with the seasons, and so he no longer runs the danger of exposing himself to fresh dangers and rival tribes with each migration. At the same time, he loses some of the freedom of the hunter.

While he bends nature to his purpose, the farming man becomes himself dependent on his land. Whereas the hunter-gatherer could always draw on the bank of natural foods the farmer depends completely on his crops and his animals. He is even more dependent than the hunter on the changes of the climate. And the more he specializes, the more dependent he becomes. Subsistence farmers tend more and more to grow the crops that produce a lot of food easily, until they reach the stage of the peasant who is growing only rice, corn or potatoes. If this crop fails, then the peasant starves. Equally important, by depending on only one or two crops he runs a much greater risk of malnutrition than does the hunter.

Furthermore, as the population increases, the pressure increases toward subsistence farming, the tendency being to grow more and more of the bulky carbohydrate crops. One can see the pattern being repeated today in many poor countries, where the large farm becomes divided among several sons or the members of a cooperative group. The nomadic herdsman needs twenty-five acres of land to feed his family, the medieval European peasant managed on one and a half acres, but an Indian peasant is forced to subsist on half an acre. Even on as little land as this, however, there is no need for a family living in a warm climate to suffer from malnutrition. How it fares depends on the efficiency of the farming, the amount of fertilizer used, the amount of rainfall and the crops planted. Let us look at some examples.

In the mountains of northern Mexico live the Tarahumara, an Indian tribe related to the Apaches. They have been in the same part of Mexico for about one thousand years, but since the coming of the Spanish and the increase in the number of *mestizos* (half-castes), the tribe has retreated farther into the mountains, giving up much of their fertile land in the valleys. Like their ancestors before them, they live a life that is partly hunting and partly farming. The land they inhabit is rocky, with thin soil, over five thousand feet above sea level. Much of it is covered with pine woods, but in the more fertile valleys, where the soil is a little deeper, farming can be carried on. Running up into the mountains, three thousand feet below the people's customary habitat, are the canyons. The climate there is much warmer, and the Tarahumara move down into these canyons when the winter becomes too severe in the hills. Most of their year, however, is spent at the high altitudes.

THE NATURAL LIFE: MAN THE FARMER

In 1971 I spent a few weeks in the Tarahumara country and saw the way they lived. They are a profoundly conservative tribe, who have kept to their own ways and their own language in the face of the advancing Spanish-Mexican culture. Each family lives in its own log cabin, with its own plot of land where corn and beans are grown. These form the staple diet, but they are supplemented by leaves, berries and roots of wild plants, as well as the occasional deer hunted in the pine woods. The Tarahumara could not be called a successful people in the economic sense, because, rather like the bushmen, they have been pushed back onto the least hospitable land, but they have retained a considerable degree of freedom. This is a conscious choice on their part, for it would be easy for them to raise their standard of living, in the economic sense, by learning Spanish, intermarrying and taking work in other parts of the country.

Although it is now being eroded by outside influences, we must assume that the Tarahumara have stuck to their traditional way of life because it offers them something that gives them more satisfaction than the Mexican culture. The most striking thing about them is their tribal sport, which replaces the dancing and magic rituals found in other tribes. This sport is called *rarajipari*—the kick-ball game—and it has been in existence since before the Spanish conquest at least. It is a form of relay race, but instead of a baton a team member passes on a small wooden ball by flicking it forward with his toes. The next member of the team, running ahead, gathers the ball with his foot and flicks it another twenty or thirty yards to the man ahead of him, while the man at the back runs up to the front. The game is contested by two teams, over the rough hill tracks through the pine woods. The course is over a fixed number of laps, which generally run from one settlement to another and back again, and the total distance of a race is never less than fifty miles and may be over a hundred and fifty miles. The race is run nonstop, day and night.

This sport has a central place in the lives of the Tarahumara, the best runners enjoying the highest prestige in the villages. Large quantities of goods—skirts, blankets, pots and pans—are bet on the results. The preparation of the runners before the race and their feeding during it are subjects of great skill and mystery, and magic is employed both in protecting the team and in getting at the opposition. The whole contest demands tremendous stamina, skill and dedication.

The significant thing about this is that this Indian tribe, living in beautiful but inhospitable surroundings, often close to the lower level of subsistence, has created an all-embracing culture system based on sport. This sport is closely linked to hunting, in that it requires many of the same qualities for success: it provides a goal for the "warrior" class; it affords the drama of the hunt and it binds the tribe together by giving them a common involvement. As a by-product, it also produces some of the greatest feats of physical endurance seen anywhere in the world.

The Tarahumara cannot be called supermen, but the degree of fitness, both muscular and cardiovascular, of the older men and women is far higher than it is among their "civilized" counterparts. Like the nomads and the hunters, they are prone to infectious diseases, particularly bronchial troubles and eye infections. Over the next few decades it will be interesting to see whether the availability of medical treatment, allied to their fitness, does enable them to live to a great age.

When we move from the Tarahumara to the more typical peasant farmer, we are considering a very large proportion of the world's population, which makes it harder than usual to generalize. In the underdeveloped countries the greater proportion of the people live by subsistence agriculture. This is the life, tied to the land, that so many city dwellers idealize as the "natural life." Yet in most respects the peasant farmer has lost the advantages of one world without gaining anything in return. Overcrowding has forced more and more people to live on the available land, a situation typically found in India, where the members of a family till a plot so small that all they can afford to grow is a carbohydrate crop, such as rice or millet. This gives them barely enough calories to live on and leaves them with protein and mineral deficiencies. In this situation such phrases as "lack of stress" and "being in tune with nature" are meaningless. Overcrowding without wealth means lack of sanitation, infestation with parasites and spread of infectious diseases. With the population already weakened by malnutrition, the infantile death rate is high and the life expectancy low. Exercise there may be, but this is limited by a diet low in calories. Without enough protein in the diet, the rebuilding of muscles in response to exercise cannot occur.

Having made this observation, let us consider whether the farming life could have anything to offer. Examples of extreme longevity, for instance, come mostly from agricultural communities, the best-known being those from Georgia, in the Soviet Union. A similar community studied recently lives in the Andes, in a village called Vilcabamba. To explain the remarkable longevity of the villagers, the tendency has been to take one aspect of their life and hold it up as the prescription for a long life. For example, the Andean villagers eat meat rarely—this is held up by vegetarians as proof that meat is a poison; they are said to have a low total caloric consumption—this is maintained as proof that no one needs more than twenty-five hundred calories a day.

In the absence of suitable "controls," the scientific attitude must be that the longevity of the villagers of Vilcabamba is due to a combination of genetic, nutritional and environmental factors. However, only patient analysis and controlled experimentation—which with humans, even if permitted, would take five hundred years—could give us a definite answer. There is not yet a secret of eternal youth, but if we could put ourselves in the situation of these centenarians, we might be able to get some of the benefits they get.

Probably the most important thing to do, if you want to be a hundred years old, is pick the right parents, who will give you the genes for longevity. If you live in an isolated mountain village that has cold winters you will escape the infectious diseases that spread through the more populated and insect-ridden lowlands. Living in your village, avoiding wars and diseases, you need also to strike the balance between over- and underfeeding. In the mountains, with intercommunication difficult, the size of the village remains stable;

there is enough food for all, but not much surplus. The other thing you must get right is your exercise level. This is where the agricultural life can have its benefits. In a mountain community, farming is always mixed—that is to say, both stock and crops. If you are looking after cattle, goats or llamas, you are going to spend a good deal of time trekking up and down the hillsides. Working on the land is good exercise, but too much digging and too much carrying of heavy loads lead to backache, and loss of spinal mobility. With a mixed farm there is therefore a balance of digging with walking, as well as a balance of protein and dairy products with carbohydrate foods.

Lastly, the dwellers in small mountain communities enjoy a balanced mental life, with its share of pleasures as well as its share of stresses. In the villages of Georgia, where the habits of the centenarians were studied, what most impressed me was the extent to which the old people were involved in the life of the village. They were running their own farms and even remarrying at the age of ninety. They were not "retiring" or stagnating, but going on leading a full life. Most of the centenarians were married, some of them more than once; most of them took alcohol or smoked cheroots, or both. Of course this does not prove that you need to drink alcohol to live to be a hundred, but it does suggest to me that alcohol is not destructive if treated in the right way. (If it were, then one would expect the proportion of teetotalers to be higher among the very old than among the population as a whole.) By "the right way," I mean using the alcohol, or the cigar, as a social lubricant—to ease tensions, loosen tongues, break down hostilities, or perhaps to release aggressions. I have no scientific justification for saying this, but I feel that some loosening of the inhibitions is occasionally a very good thing.

Can these benefits be transposed into our own setting? Relatively isolated communities can still be found even in industrialized nations, but the sense of total involvement has gone. It is primarily up to the individual now to maintain his interest and enthusiasm for life after the age when society considers him fit to be pensioned off.

THE NATURAL LIFE: MAN THE FARMER

All we are left with from the agricultural life is the sense of rhythm that comes from living with the land—the sense of recurring patterns. An understanding of the world around you and an understanding of yourself will not make your life longer, but I believe it will make it more satisfactory.

At the very end of this consideration comes the modern farmer, who has a large sum of capital tied up in the land and wishes to secure an economic return. He is forced to compromise with nature in order to get results, but he is unlikely to get much health benefit. The physical work; the balanced, just adequate diet; the commitment to the community; the sense of natural rhythms—all these are absent from the pattern of his life. The mechanized one-crop farmer, necessary as he may be, belongs to the next chapter.

The author at the height of his career in 1963, competing at *Turku*, *Finland*. (The runner trailing him is Artur Hannemann of East Germany.)

The perfect way to run—with company and in beautiful surroundings. Above, the author and his son Clive. Below, the whole Tulloh family, from left to right, Sue, Josephine, Clive, Bruce, and Catherine in 1976.

Above, the author running with a Tarahumara native in the mountains of northern Mexico. The Tarahumara work the least hospitable land and are economically hard-pressed, but their surroundings are beautiful and they have a remarkably high average degree of fitness.

The Tarahumara have kept very much to their traditional ways, which include sport as an important part of their culture. Rarajipari, the kick-ball game being played below, is really a form of relay race. It is also one of the world's most demanding athletic contests.

The Masai of East Africa enjoy an excellent general state of health despite what could be called a "high-risk" diet. Another East African tribe, the Samburu, shown below, are nomads who think little of covering thirty to forty miles a day on foot. Although their diet is high in cholesterol, they suffer little cardiovascular disease.

The author reaches Phoenix, Arizona, on his transcontinental run in 1969. (It is possible, if not very pleasant, for anyone to run in downtown areas.) Below, he gets some moral support—and a little refreshment—from his wife, Sue.

Circuit training, an organized course of exercises, can provide excellent and convenient indoor training. This is one element, the alternate press. (see page 177)

The finish line. The author arriving in New York via ferryboat after the long run from Los Angeles in 1969.

3

The Unnatural Life: Urban Man

And so we come to civilized man. Perhaps "urban man" is the better term, for some aspects of city life are certainly not civilized. We have not been crowding ourselves into cities for very long. The first city dwellers in Mesopotamia and the Nile basin, between seven and ten thousand years ago, formed only a small fraction of the population. It might be true to say that real city life began with Rome, and I suspect that a study of Roman medical records would reveal the onset of some of the "civilized" diseases that doctors are up against today. However, the problems did not really proliferate until the nineteenth century, when mechanical conveyance began. Before that time even the ruling classes spent a good deal of their day walking or riding—using their bodies. Only the very richest and most decadent escaped exercise by having servants and carriages to transport them, and it was among them that the diseases of affluence—obesity and high blood pressure—naturally occurred. The fate of the urban poor in Europe was not unlike that of the agricultural poor discussed in the last chapter: malnutrition, infectious diseases, deaths in childbirth and low life expectancy.

With the improvements in agriculture, trade and building, the life expectancy and the numbers of the population rose in Europe, though checked by the occasional ravages of plague. Villages became towns, and towns cities. The steady growth of business suddenly became a surge in the nineteenth century with the development of the iron and coal industries and the import of cheap raw materials from overseas colonies. Factories sprang up, workers flooded in from the country to live in what were often squalid housing conditions and the modern pattern of ill health and disease took shape.

In the tenements of industrial Europe the standard of health was, if anything, worse than in the preindustrial period. The quality of food was low—the first efforts at mass production for large populations produced some horrifying additives—and infections spread in the crowded conditions. The common diseases were tuberculosis, typhoid, cholera, scarlet fever, smallpox and diphtheria. However, the profit motive provided some relief. Employers, both philanthropic and self-interested, developed housing schemes; railway travel enabled people to live farther away from their work in more spacious, suburban surroundings; company doctors started medical inspections; local governments installed sewers. Soap became cheaper and more people washed—both themselves and their clothes. And as wages increased, people were able to afford adequate food. By 1881 the average life expectancy in Europe had risen to forty-five.

In the last part of the nineteenth century the great medical advances started to have their effects. Many disease-causing organisms were identified and immunization techniques were employed. By 1920, the average life expectancy in the United States reached 54.1 years; by 1940, 62 years, and by 1967, 70.5 years.

If death rates for certain diseases were the same today as in the year 1900, almost 400,000 Americans would lose their lives to tuberculosis, almost 300,000 to gastroenteritis, 80,000 to diphtheria and 55,000 to poliomyelitis. Instead, the toll from all four diseases is now less than 10,000 lives a year. Gains in combating the once-great killers, which also included typhoid fever, smallpox and plague, have been achieved by both treatment and prevention—the former, with antibacterial drugs; the latter, with improvements in nutrition and sanitation as well as immunization.

In view of all this we ought to be perfectly healthy, but we are not. Very rarely does anyone die of "old age"; not only do we die before the end of our possible span, but we suffer during a very large part of our life from the accumulating effects of what are called the "degenerative diseases." These are diseases caused by the body's own malfunction, with little or no help from invading pathogens. It is here that we must start helping ourselves.

The medical profession is chronically overstretched in trying to patch up or halt the results of degeneration that has reached a dangerous level. Enormous amounts of money are spent on equipment for treating the hearts, lungs, kidneys and digestive systems of those who are already degenerating. Not a single nation has yet instituted a program for preventing these diseases, in spite of the fact that the money spent on prevention would be far outweighed by the money saved. The first thing that must happen is that people must realize *their* responsibility for *their own* health and disease. In Samuel Butler's *Erewhon* those who committed crimes were sent to hospitals and those who became ill were sent to prison. We have now advanced to the understanding that much crime springs from mental ill health; the next step is to appreciate the extent of our responsibility for our own physical health. An even older example that we might do well to follow is the reputed practice of the ancient Chinese, who paid their doctors when they were healthy and stopped paying them when they became ill. Although one certainly cannot accuse the ordinary practitioner of having a financial interest in our ill health, there is no doubt that specialists are far more interested, for purely professional reasons, in the sick than in the healthy.

The time may come when every neighborhood has a medical screening center that can monitor everyone's state of health every year or half-year, but in the meantime it is up to us to look after ourselves—not merely to avoid an early death but to get the best out of life. Statistics will show how many people are dying of diseases they could have avoided, but they will not show that vast gray area of people who are not fully healthy. How many people are taking some kind of pain-killer, tranquilizer or stimulant because they do not feel as well as they ought? How many are suffering from depression or neurosis? How many have to live life at half-throttle because of bad feet, poor digestion or strained backs?

A recent survey of a typical group of American households found that the number of medicines on hand ranged up to 88, with a mean of 30. Yearly, more than $300,000,000 is spent in advertising drug products on television. U.S. pharmaceutical production data show a doubling of consumption of prescription drugs over the past ten years! A single drug, a tranquilizer (Valium), which ranks as the largest-selling prescription drug in America, was consumed at the rate of three billion tablets in 1974.

I would venture to say that of the twenty-five million men and women in Britain over the age of forty, not more than one-tenth are really healthy—and I see no reason to doubt that that would be equally true in America. Even if one-fifth or one-third are properly fit, many millions are left who could be living much more enjoyable and more active lives.

The leading causes of death in the United States are as follows:

TABLE 2   MAJOR CAUSES OF DEATH

Cause	Annual Deaths
Heart disease	745,360
Cancer	318,910
Cerebrovascular disease	209,420
Accidents	111,460
Influenza and pneumonia	69,750
Diabetes	38,470
Emphysema and bronchitis	30,540
Cirrhosis of the liver	28,910

Let us consider first what these diseases are and what can be done to avoid them. Although this is common knowledge, it has to be repeated: if one person reading this book is moved to do something about his or her physical condition, then I shall have achieved something.

If we rule out cancer and accidents, this still leaves over 1,120,000 deaths that might have been avoided or delayed by better physical condition.

Although it is not strictly within my domain, I might add that many of the cancer deaths might have been also avoidable, had the victims taken sufficient interest in their own condition to have themselves checked at an earlier date. Cancer is not necessarily a killer, and the earlier it is treated the more likely is a complete cure.

However, I should like to deal with the diseases that are actually avoidable by a sensible way of life. The diseases that are the most important in this category are heart disease and cerebrovascular diseases (stroke). A notable fact about them is that they occur far, far more commonly in civilized societies than in primitive communities. There is now a mass of data, some of which I have already quoted, showing the absence of hypertension (a major factor in coronary heart disease, heart failure, heart attack, stroke and kidney disease) in primitive tribes such as the Samburu of Kenya, the islanders in Micronesia, the Kalahari bushmen and the Amazonian Indians. There is also plenty of evidence that as civilization spreads, so the incidence of the "civilized" diseases increases. In Puerto Rico, the death rates from heart disease have increased steadily over the past fifteen years. In Johannesburg, South Africa, myocardial infarction (heart attack) is common among the wealthy white population but rare among the Bantu. In Africa as a whole, hypertension and myocardial infarction are rare in the Negro population; they are increasingly common, however, among American blacks.

In these tribes in Kenya, not only is there a low incidence of hypertension but there is no increase with age as occurs in the United States. However, it has been noted that when the young men of the tribe are conscripted into the armed services, there are slight increases in their blood pressure.

THE UNNATURAL LIFE: URBAN MAN

The associated group of troubles—hardening of the arteries, heart disease and strokes—are attributed by the medical profession to a number of factors for which there is statistical support. These are, in no particular order, excess cholesterol in the blood, elevated blood pressure, overeating, lack of exercise, smoking and stress. The connection between excess weight and heart trouble is now so well established that some insurance companies demand higher premiums from individuals who are more than ten percent above the prescribed weight level for their height and build. Both obesity and high serum cholesterol are directly linked with the amount of food that a person eats. A study in Framingham, Massachusetts, which has been following five thousand residents of that community for more than twenty years has established that those who were thirty percent overweight were two and a half times as likely to develop a coronary thrombosis as those of normal weight, and other studies have shown that those smoking twenty cigarettes a day had almost twice as much chance of an attack as the non-smokers.

Numerous studies have shown a close correlation between the amount of exercise a man gets in his employment and the incidence of heart disease. One study by Dr. J. N. Morris in Britain found that drivers of London double-decker buses, who were seated all day, had half again as many heart attacks as did the conductors, who were walking about and running up and down stairs all day. A study by Dr. Daniel Brunner in Israel showed sedentary workers in a kibbutz with two and a half to four times the rate of fatal coronaries of the active workers. One American study of 120,000 railroad employees revealed a heart-attack incidence among sedentary office workers almost twice that for men working in the yards. Another of postal workers found that excess risk of heart attacks for clerks was 1.4 to 1.9 times that for letter carriers.

One of the ways in which exercise brings benefits is directly in the reduction of serum cholesterol. A study by Dr. Lawrence A. Golding of Kent State University showed that an exercise program conducted with a large group over a period of months brought about a twenty-five-percent drop in the serum cholesterol level compared with an untrained group. At Camp Lejeune, North Carolina, 100 marines in rigorous training were fed at least 4,500 calories a day in a diet deliberately made rich with saturated fat. At the end of six months of heavy eating but also of continuous hard work, their blood fats and weights were unchanged. Let us now consider the causes and prevention of these troubles in more detail.

DIET

National surveys in the United States suggest that forty-eight million Americans may have severe nutritional deficiencies and another twenty-four million may have deficiencies classed as "serious." Lack of variety in food can lead to a deficiency of vitamins and minerals. A more common fault in the average diet is an excess of sugar and foods made with sugar—candies, cookies, cakes, pastries, sweet drinks. The sugar contains plenty of calories, of course, but it contains nothing else—no protein, no fat, no vitamins. Even the greediest ease up on their food when they have exceeded their daily caloric needs, so if those calories have been composed mostly of sugar foods their diet may be lacking in some essentials. Sugar is not in itself bad—it is simply not enough. Most of the athletes I know take a lot of sugar in their drinks and eat chocolate cookies, but these are only as extras to the normal diet, and they help to put back the extra thousand calories that the serious athlete is using each day. When I ran across the United States I was burning up about six thousand calories a day, and I ate a vast amount of sweet foods to put those back—sweet tea and strawberry-jam sandwiches, pancakes with syrup, ice cream. I also took care to eat plenty of fresh fruit and vegetables and enough meat, cheese and egg protein.

As well as consuming too much sugar, most people simply eat too much, and this leads to their putting on weight. There is an answer to this—one exercise that will infallibly lessen your weight problem. The lips are closed, and the head is moved from side to side. This exercise should be repeated whenever you are offered a second helping of potatoes or dessert.

I am not going to lay down hard-and-fast rules about diet. For one thing, it would restrict the enjoyment of food, which I consider to be one of life's greatest pleasures; for another, no diet plan can take into account the wide range of foods available. Looking around the world one can see people managing to stay fit with drastically different eating habits—some entirely vegetarian, some almost without vegetable foods. Even on the question of cholesterol and animal fats, about which I shall say more later, it is impossible to be dogmatic. One diet rule on which most doctors are agreed, however, is the need to have some fibrous food, or "roughage," in the daily diet. This roughage, which may be a fibrous vegetable like cabbage or the wheat husks in whole-grain bread, does two things. It gives something for the muscles of the intestine to push on, because it is not liquefied like processed foods, and it prevents all the water from being reabsorbed into the large intestine as the food approaches the end of the alimentary canal. This means that toxic compounds present in foods do not stay in the intestines for days or even weeks, but are pushed along through the body and gotten rid of in less than forty-eight hours.

In deciding whether you are eating the right kinds of food, and the right amounts, there is no need to count up all the calories that you take in and the number of calories that you use up. You must just check your weight regularly, and if it shows a measurable rise then you are either eating too much or exercising too little. See Chapter 7 for more details. If you have to cut down on the amounts, do so gradually, so that eating less becomes a habit. If you cut out a meal completely it will just upset the natural rhythm of the body and probably result in a lowering of your blood sugar, making you feel miserable, so that you will then abandon the "dieting" attempts and go back to the same old ways.

It is better to exercise more rather than to eat less—if you can manage it. An extra twenty-minute run or set of exercises will use up another three hundred calories, about a tenth of your daily intake.

If you really have to restrict your diet, then start by following these simple rules:

1. Don't eat unless you are hungry, and when you start feeling full, stop.
2. Eat meat not more than twice a day, and vary it with fish, eggs or cheese dishes as alternatives.
3. Never eat fried foods twice in a day.
4. Have some fresh fruit or, failing that, fruit juice every day.
5. Never have a protein dish (meat, fish, eggs) without accompanying it with a vegetable dish, the fresher the better.
6. Don't become a slave to coffee, tea or alcohol. Have one day in the week when you drink no alcohol at all.
7. If you have to cut down, cut down on the sugar, starchy foods and alcohol and eat plenty of the rest.

If you follow these guidelines you will get sufficient vitamins and minerals from the fruit and vegetables, sufficient fat and sufficient protein. Getting enough carbohydrate foods to provide the additional calories is never a problem, because such basic foods as bread, cereals and potatoes all provide them in large amounts, while sugar and alcohol provide further calories.

When you are exercising regularly, you will find that you do not overeat as you might suppose. The fit body is a much more efficient self-regulator than the unfit body, and it will become full, particularly if you are including the roughage foods, when you have eaten enough. If you really do overeat, tempted by something delicious, you will feel overfull when you next go out training, and the feeling of discomfort will (or should) make you cut down the following day.

The effect of continual overeating—increased weight—harms the body in several ways. First, the extra body weight means that your heart has to work harder. Second, the additional fat will tend to conserve your body heat, which is fine if you are an Eskimo but very uncomfortable on a hot day in the United States. Finally, the increased level of fat in the body leads to an increased possibility of hardening of the arteries, through fatty substances' being deposited on the walls of the blood vessels.

Having said that, let me not put you off from enjoying your food. My wife is a very good cook and I enjoy doing justice to her cooking, but if I know I am going to eat a big meal I cut down a bit on the one before and perhaps take a little bit more exercise that day.

One harmful effect of civilized foods, particularly sugary foods, whether eaten in excess or not, is the dental decay they cause. The side effects of bad teeth may in turn affect the general health by causing infections, resulting in sore throats or tonsillitis. This dental decay is not found among the few true hunter-gatherer tribes that survive, because they are using their teeth in the way for which they evolved: chewing up tough, uncooked food. This chewing of a wide variety of vegetable foods, as well as tough meat, keeps the gums healthy and prevents food from accumulating between the teeth. The only replacement for this is a lot of brushing, after every meal.

Diet is important; as Magnus Pyke has said, "We are what we eat." There have been many books written on caloric output and intake, and it would be a waste of time to repeat the arguments here. However, I have included charts, at the end of the book, showing the caloric content of common foods and the approximate caloric expenditure of a number of daily activities. This should be sufficient for any enthusiastic weight watcher armed with an electronic calculator!

BLOOD PRESSURE, STRESS AND EXERCISE

I want now to discuss the complex problems of the heart, stress and exercise. Although the subject is a vast one, on

51

which a lot of research is still being done, the messages that emerge for us are fairly simple.

Let us start with the facts, already pointed out, that many primitive peoples do not suffer from increasingly high blood pressure with age. It is considered normal in European and American society for the blood pressure to increase in this way.

Some people have a natural tendency to higher blood pressure than others, as do certain physical types: high pressure is more commonly found in the short and stocky than in the long and lean. Excessively high blood pressure is regarded as dangerous, because it may result in damage to the heart or stroke, leading to death of brain cells and hence to paralysis and death.

In the natural state, several changes take place when the body is placed on an "emergency footing"—for instance, before a hunt or a battle. There is an increase in the secretion of adrenaline into the bloodstream, an increase in the viscosity of the blood, an increase in the heart rate and the blood pressure and an increase in the blood sugar, as some of the stored glucose in the liver is released. When exercise starts, the blood is diverted away from the stomach and liver, and more flows to the muscles that are being used. The increased flow of blood is needed by the muscles, as is the extra blood sugar. When exercise is taking place, there is a rise in the blood pressure as the heartbeat increases, but then it falls again as the capillaries in the working muscles open up.

In urban man, however, the surge of adrenaline that is caused by anger, excitement or terror is not, as a rule, followed by a chase or battle. The heart is pumping the blood harder, but the muscles are not being used. Tension may build within the body and contribute to chronic elevation of blood pressure.

Stress also can contribute to elevation of blood cholesterol levels. In studies at the University of Oklahoma in which diet, exercise and other factors were held constant, with only emotional stress changing, marked increases in cholesterol level were measured when stress increased.

If blood cholesterol level is high, some of the cholesterol may be laid down along with fats on the inner walls of arteries so that the arteries gradually harden and narrow, impeding blood flow and making it easier for the vessels to be blocked completely by clots. The hardening-and-narrowing process is aided, some investigators believe, by high blood pressure, which, in effect, may pound the fats and cholesterol into the artery walls.

Excess weight enters the picture—in more than one way. When eating exceeds what is needed—when caloric intake is greater than caloric expenditure—the body starts to store fats. This leads to a rise in fat in the bloodstream. There may also be an excess of cholesterol in the diet. Cholesterol is not a poison. It is a substance that the body needs, and if you are not getting enough, more of it will be synthesized in your liver. The trouble starts when a high animal-fat intake, containing cholesterol, is combined with a high carbohydrate intake and lack of sufficient exercise. Although the Masai live almost entirely on animal products, they do not suffer from hardening of the arteries. This is probably because they take plenty of exercise and eat very small amounts of starchy or sugary foods.

We thus have a multiple series of hazards in the urban man, with his hardening arteries; with his increasing weight, which contributes to elevation of blood pressure, which in turn contributes to hardening of the arteries; and with surges of unreleased aggressiveness or fear placing sudden additional strain on the vascular system. All of this can be avoided by adherence to the natural life. Correct diet and exercise habits can do much to prevent arteriosclerosis and hypertension, but what should you do about the stress? The adrenaline secretion is a preparation for action, for movement, so this is the natural course to take. In a situation of frustration you must relieve your frustrations with violent exercise. It is better to jump up and down with rage than to bottle it up, and if you get home through the rush-hour traffic seething with indignation, get outside and run hard. When Rudyard Kipling said, "If you can fill the unforgiving minute / With sixty seconds' worth of distance run . . ." he was absolutely right.

It is obvious that whatever steps we take toward a more natural way of life should be those that will contribute toward an increase in the exercise level, a balanced and not excessive diet and a release of frustrations.

Just as damaging as short-term frustration is long-term stress. We know that stress can be produced by many different causes—illness, shock, heavy physical exercise or emotional strain. What is interesting is that the body responds in the same way whatever the cause of the stress. Although we may suggest steps by which stress may be avoided, it will always be with us, and of course it always has been with us. The human body needs some stress in order to make its adjustments to the surrounding world. A being brought up without any stress at all is a cabbage; but a being subjected to too much stress will break down, become less resistant to infection, more subject to nervous diseases and more prone to the heart and blood-pressure problems mentioned above.

What we need, as in most of life, is a balance—a controlled amount of stress that will train our bodies to withstand stress, just as we can train our muscles to work harder. In the old days the various stages of initiation and introduction to the ways of the tribe brought a gradually increasing degree of physical and mental pressure. The assumptions behind some of the more spartan systems of education and training are based on the same tribal instinct. Body and mind are linked; the mental pressure caused by fear of an ordeal can affect the hormone system just as much as the strenuous ordeal itself. The body that has undergone stresses, up to a certain level, will be better able to withstand stress in the future. By measuring the response of the adrenal cortex to a stimulating hormone, and by looking for traces of certain hormones in the urine, it is possible to measure stress levels and the individual's adaptation to them, but the procedure is too complex to be in widespread use. We have to rely on judgment and experience in knowing how much stress a recruit, an athlete or a child can take. This is where the use of graduated doses of exercise comes in, something I shall say more about in Chapter 6.

4

Understanding Yourself

Everybody wants to know what to do. Whether consciously or not, we all look for signposts, or follow pathways that others have made. We travel one journey from birth to death, never able to retrace our steps, never quite repeating ourselves and never knowing what lies round the next corner. Everybody has to learn for himself how to cope with the changes in his life; nobody has quite the same set of experiences and nobody else is quite like you.

It is a genetical fact that everybody is unique. Even identical twins, who start off with the same set of genes, will differ slightly as life works on them in different ways. The starting point of healthy self-respect is this realization that you are unique. You are a complex of mind and body—at the same time the highest form of life on earth and a system of cells, tissues, blood, bones and hormones that follow biological patterns. Having powers of reason, you are capable of changing your fate and your future. It is up to you what you make of yourself. Doctors and authors, priests, parents and psychiatrists will give advice, but it is your nature that will decide the course of action.

You will notice that I said "your nature," rather than "your mind" or "your brain." Many decisions are not consciously made, and many actions are not based on decisions at all, but on feelings, and feelings depend on the state of your body as well as your mind. Indeed, the use of pure reason influences us much less than our built-in desires and acquired prejudices. What kind of person you will develop into depends on what actions you take, and these depend on your present state of mind and body. This in turn depends on what has happened to you in the past and the nature you were born with.

Most people go through life as programmed as a washing machine. The habits of their childhood and the early patterns of behavior prevent them from developing fully. To take a crude example, a child of fat parents who has been encouraged to eat a lot when young is likely to grow fat. Being in a fat family, he believes that fatness is good, and being fat, he will take little exercise. Through not taking enough exercise he will continue to grow fat, and, being fat, he will die before his time. To break out of this cycle requires two things: understanding and the exercise of free will.

What I want to give you in this book is the understanding of your bodily nature. And once you can understand the principles on which your body operates, you can understand causes and effects. If a man had a car and thought it worked on the principle of a steam engine, he would make some pretty stupid decisions. People do equally stupid things to their bodies.

We are animals; there is no denying it. A skinned man looks very much like a skinned rabbit and even more like a skinned monkey. To put us all on a still more basic level, a human cell when dividing behaves in the same way as the cell of a tadpole or an earthworm. The laws of genetics were worked out with peas and fruit flies and the structure of the gene is being worked out with bacteria and viruses, yet they all hold good for man. There is something comforting about this, I think. We are not in the position of being God's chosen creatures, loaded with guilt and threatened by devils. We are just the highest form of life that has so far developed on this particular planet. There are other planets, other suns, other galaxies and there must be life elsewhere, but we have to make do with ourselves.

Life has been evolving on earth for more than a billion years. How long man has been on the scene is at the moment still in doubt. The skull, dated at two million years old, discovered by Richard Leakey near Lake Rudolf, in Kenya, is that of some kind of human, not of an ape-man, and there may be hominid skulls even older than that. Compared with our written history, our biological history is very long indeed, and it is this which has shaped us.

I can hear people saying that this is irrelevant, that man is changing continually and that he adapts to new situations. To emphasize how much we are conditioned by our past I must spend a little time explaining how evolution works. When an embryo is developing, the pattern of its development is controlled by the genes. These genes are carried in the nucleus of each cell, and each time the cell divides the complete set of genes is copied. When an animal grows up and reproduces, the sperm and the egg cells each contain half a set of genes, and when the sperm fertilizes the egg the number of genes in the cell is restored to normal. Each new individual gets half a set of genes from its mother and half from its father, but the makeup of these half-sets varies greatly. The number of genes runs into thousands, so all individuals will be slightly different. Moreover, during the process of gene copying and reproduction, changes, called mutations, sometimes occur in the genes.

We therefore have the situation in which very slight differences, small differences working over a very long period of time, are constantly appearing in a species. The process of natural selection operates on this "gene pool," favoring some genes at the expense of others. It does this because the animals that have useful variations will tend to survive and breed, whereas the ones without these variations will have a slightly lower chance of survival and therefore a lower breeding rate. The advantages that are favored will depend on the environment. If the climate became colder over a period of, say, ten thousand years, animals with thick coats would tend to be selected. Genes that caused increased growth would be an advantage to a horse, in enabling it to run faster, and in fact, over a period of fifty million years, the size of the horse has gradually increased, as can be seen from fossils.

In many species evolution seems to have stopped. When the animal is perfectly suited to its environment, new variations can only be disadvantageous, and the form of the animal may remain the same for millions of years, or even, as we can see in some fishes, reptiles and insects, for hundreds of millions of years. But if the environment undergoes a sudden change, then there may be rapid selection of certain features in only a few generations.

What has happened with man? He is a very slow breeder compared with most animals, with only about four generations per hundred years, as against twenty or thirty generations for other large mammals. This is one factor tending to slow down his rate of evolution. Another factor is that his mobility and intelligence have enabled him to mold the environment to suit himself, rather than the other way round. It is for this reason that the Eskimo, although they have lived in the Arctic for thousands of years, have not grown coats like polar bears. They have undergone slight changes in body shape, but they are still the same species as the Karamojong on the edge of Lake Victoria.

Even more important than this, ever since man developed his high intelligence he has been capable of controlling his own evolution—that is, controlling which babies should survive and which should be killed. He has eliminated those with physical deformities or any that differed from the normal. The only mutations that would have survived would be those which gave an advantage, but which were not physically obvious. One such was the gene that gave partial protection against malaria; it has spread itself through the malarial countries. Genes for intelligence would come into this category, so it is possible that we are more intelligent than our distant ancestors.

In this century the situation has changed. The advances in medicine and hygiene have permitted far more children to survive who would otherwise have been killed off by disease. Natural selection has ceased to operate in this sector, and it is true to say that by helping the weak and disabled to survive and possibly to breed, we are in fact tending to weaken our genetic stock slightly. Some weaknesses, which would previously have been eliminated, will undoubtedly be passed on. However, the number of such cases is small compared with the total number of births, and to have any genetic effect on our pool of genes they would take scores of generations, not just one or two. In the meantime we may actually be preserving some potentially advantageous genes that could help the human race to survive a global calamity.

The genetic position today is that we possess the same genes, mixed up but basically unchanged, as our ancestors had twenty generations ago. Twenty generations is nothing on the scale of evolution—a mere blink in time. Consider two thousand generations—fifty thousand years. There has been a little change since that time, when Neanderthal Man was being replaced by Cro-Magnon Man, but not much. The skeleton is essentially the same as ours. There have been slight differences in proportion, such as the recession of the browridge of the Neanderthal; but the height and musculature of the Cro-Magnon men would not make them seem out of place in a modern swimming pool, and from their skull size, their brains were as good as ours.

What evolutionary pressures have been working on humans since those days? Out of those two thousand generations, physical ability has been an important factor in survival for about nineteen hundred and ninety generations. I don't mean just physical strength or quickness with the spear, but the ability to survive the day-to-day life, with its exposure to hunger, disease, extremes of temperature and the blows of fate. The human body, therefore, is not something that is going to snap as soon as a little stress is applied to it. You have the body of a caveman—or cavewoman. That may not seem the case when you look at yourself in the mirror, but it is true. The body you inherited from your ancestors is capable, if need be, of living the kind of life they lived, and what is more, it needs the kind of exercise they took in order to function properly.

NATURAL FITNESS

What do we do? We protect the caveman's body against disease, by washing and by medical care. That is fine. We keep it warm inside clothes, heated buildings and heated cars. That is fine too. It seems likely, from his lack of hair, his sweat glands and his diet, that man evolved in a hot climate, so there is nothing unnatural about that. There is no virtue in cold air and cold baths for their own sake. Where we go wrong is in pampering and overfeeding the body. We are hunting animals. No one who had an expensive pedigreed hound would treat it like a lapdog. In order to be kept in condition it needs regular exercise, food and sleep.

I can sense that the last paragraph has upset a good few people. "Here comes another of those killjoy fitness fanatics," you say; "it'll be two pieces of Melba toast and a slice of lemon for supper." That is not the case. I shall say more about diet and about my philosophy later on, but I want to make it clear that I am on the side of the Epicureans. I enjoy my life. I very seldom do anything I don't want to do. I know that by living the right way I can get more out of every day than the unfit person, and it grieves me to see people wasting themselves.

I am preaching a doctrine of exercise, but that does not mean suffering. There are some people who have to be forced to take exercise and who suffer genuinely in the process, but that is not surprising in view of the unnatural way many of us live. If you kept a man down in a mine for years and then brought him up to the surface, he would find the light painful; but when he became used to the light he would not go down into the mine again. That is the case with fitness. The majority of people over thirty, and many of those over twenty, have so far lost the fitness of their childhood that they cannot even remember what it was like.

I can tell you. It is the feeling of lightness, of spring in your step when you walk down the road. It is the feeling of wondering what is round the next corner and not being afraid of it. It is being able to work all day, come home and go for a half-hour five-mile run and feel refreshed by it; then to spend an hour in the garden, go to a dinner party, have a bottle of wine, dance, make love and wake up next morning looking forward to the day.

Fitness is the feeling of being in tune with the earth; when you are out in the fresh air every day, you can feel the turning of the seasons. You can sense the time of day by the change in the quality of the light; the changes in the weather come not as arbitrary acts of fate, but as predictable moods in an old friend. I have visited or lived in forty countries in my forty years, and in every one of those countries have I run. I have run through the streets of Moscow, Hong Kong and Los Angeles; I have run through the forests of Finland and Hungary, the dry and dusty plains of Australia and the African Rift Valley and through the humid warmth of Jamaica and the Camargue. Better than that, I have run on the beaches, from Braunton Burrows to Nathanya, to Ostia, to Santa Barbara, to Auckland and Perth and Mombasa. Better still, I have run on the hilltops—Ben Nevis and the Lakes, Mount Kenya and Ol Doinyo Lengai, the Alps, the Rockies and the Sierra Madre of Mexico. When I run I draw strength from the air and the ground. I take something from the land because I am experiencing something real. It is experience that comes in through all your senses and even through your feet feeling the ground under you. Sometimes you are hot, uncomfortable, sometimes you are scared, sometimes you are lost, but it is your own reality, not something you have read about or seen.

There are other benefits, too. I know that if I see another runner, anywhere, I can treat him as a friend. I know that he is somebody who does not just accept his lot, but is prepared to do something to change himself. A man may not have a talent to be an artist, an athlete or an entertainer, but if he just has the impetus to do something about his condition, then he has my respect. I do not claim that runners are any different from other men and women, but I am happy to have made a lot of friends in different places, people who can be relied upon.

There is one more thing that running has done for me, which it will not do for everyone. It has given me the taste of competition at the highest level. To step onto the track in front of a crowd is frightening and uplifting. You know that you have no way out. You are alone; you cannot have an easy game or rest on the ropes;

you depend on your heart and legs, lungs and brain—and any of them can fail you. At the same time you are making a declaration, a challenge to the world, the crowd, the other runners. "Here I am. Just try and beat me" is what you are saying. A race is a battle; your soul is locked against the rest. You go on until everybody cracks, or else you launch yourself into the last-lap desperate charge, flinging your feet at the ground, driving the arms, pulling the body forward through pain, by will alone. Few can do it, few would wish to, but you are living on a plane of rare intensity.

In a race the mind commands the body to its limits, and by doing so it extends those limits. A lesser degree of mastery can be obtained by anyone who is prepared to give himself, or herself, time. You start with the possible and work toward the impossible. You set your own goals according to your own standards and your own needs. I have had the experience, through doing it myself and through advising others, and there is no problem you will meet that has not been met by others before you.

The first and possibly the most vital steps do not involve any physical effort at all—they involve thinking and learning. Once you understand the principles of human physical adaptation you can coach yourself.

Your body is not a machine. It is far more subtle than that. Most people, however, brought up in a machine age, do regard the body as a machine—that is, if they ever think about it at all. In fact, if it were a machine most people would treat it better than they do at present. At least people appreciate that a car needs some attention besides being given fuel, and they appreciate that it needs the right kind of fuel. The poor old body is fed all sorts of fuel, often at the wrong time and in the wrong amounts, and is supposed to go on working without any looking after. "What about the doctor?" you will say. "He's there when we need him." The doctor is to the body what the tow truck is to the car: a sign of failure.

If we were living a natural life we would not need to think about the body's needs, because they would all be met in the course of our daily life. The reason for this book is that we have gotten so far away from the natural life that we no longer know what is natural and what is not. What is regarded as natural in one culture is unnatural in another. This is why we have to get back to the biological facts about our makeup.

The first thing to realize about your body is that it is self-renewing. Your blood corpuscles, your skin and your muscle cells are not old—they are quite young, because they are continually being replaced. This is the first truth to bear in mind. If a car is overused, parts become worn and break, so it is advisable not to overuse it. With the human body it is quite different: use stimulates growth and repair. It is underuse, leading to atrophy, that is to be avoided. This applies particularly to the heart, as I shall explain in the analysis of fitness in Chapter 6.

The second truth I want you to bear in mind goes by the grand name of "homeostasis." It means preserving your equilibrium, maintaining the same state, and it is a concept that affects all the responses to exercise. To take an example. If you start exercising on a warm day your body temperature will start to rise. If the cells' temperature deviates from the normal they do not work so well, so the body starts to make adjustments. More blood is pumped to the skin to be cooled down; therefore you become red in the face and legs. If this does not lower the temperature quickly enough you start to sweat, and the evaporation from the skin cools you down. There is nothing surprising about this; what is surprising is that people worry about it. They seem to think that they are unfit if they sweat a lot. It is just the body's natural homeostatic response to a situation; in fact, many good athletes perform well because they do sweat a lot and thus keep their cell temperatures closer to normal.

The same principle applies to stiffness, soreness and strains, all of which bother people when they first take up exercise. Because of the operation of the homeostatic principle, the body is very "careful" about exceeding its limits, and long before those limits are reached the body puts out warning signals. In the case of stiffness, it is a warning sign that muscles are being overused. The stiffness or swelling that results limits the use of the muscle—or it does if you have any sense—until the natural repair and renewal processes have had a chance to work.

The third concept grows out of the first two. It is the "overload response." If the muscles are put under a certain amount of strain, enough for them to feel it but not enough for any damage to be caused, then, over a matter of days, the muscles build themselves up to meet the strain. It is partly a case of the natural renewal processes' taking place—the growth of fresh muscle fibers or the development of extra lengths of blood capillaries—and partly the homeostatic principle. If one part of the body is being put under a strain that it cannot really deal with, then the body's equilibrium is upset. There is a local shortage of oxygen or a shift in the sugar or acidity level in the blood. To correct this upset to the equilibrium, we strengthen the part that was overused in order that it can deal with the extra load next time. All modern training is based on this principle—the kind of training used by track runners, swimmers, cyclists and weight lifters. It is not really new; the same principle was used by the young Hercules. He started carrying a calf around the house on his shoulders the day it was born. Every day he repeated the trip, and as the calf grew heavier he grew stronger. It was in fact a model form of progressive overload training, which we would do well to follow. The great thing about it was that the steps were very gradual, almost imperceptible. He started from something that was possible and worked on until he achieved the impossible—carrying the fully grown bull around on his shoulders.

The last concept I want to discuss is one that has so far received less attention than I think it deserves, and that is rhythm. The body does not work away at the same pace day in and day out. As most people are aware, we have our good days and our bad days. The female monthly cycle is not the only natural rhythm that affects physical performance. There are the circadian rhythms— that is to say, the rhythms that fluctuate during the twenty-four hours; longer rhythms over a period of about a month; and there is also a yearly rhythm. I am not talking about a vague "natural force," or auras or anything of that kind. I am talking about

UNDERSTANDING YOURSELF

measurable changes in the internal conditions of the body that take place according to definite patterns. For example, levels of blood pressure and blood sugar fluctuate rhythmically during the day, affecting both physical and mental performance. Other regular changes can be measured in your body temperature, your hemoglobin level, the activity of your adrenal glands and your pulse rate.

Until recently this concept was not part of general medical practice, but a lot of research has been and is being done in this area. It is likely that the present rather mechanistic view of the body will in time be replaced by a view of the whole body as a system in dynamic equilibrium—the view of doctors in medieval and ancient times. At the moment there are few guidelines; it is up to you to chart the rhythmical changes in your body.

The implications of these changes in terms of our daily lives are considerable, but I will concentrate on their application to physical well-being and performance. The regular fluctuations mean that at different times of the day your physical capacity varies. When pulse, temperature and adrenaline level are low, you tend to be sluggish; you respond less quickly, and if you have to make an effort you do not feel "full of energy." At other times of the day you feel really on the ball, full of go, able to make quick decisions and throw yourself into things. From years of experience as an athlete, training and noting my performance every day, I know very well that I perform better at certain times of day, and it came as no surprise to find that there are physiological reasons. Most of us, however, run our lives on the principle that we function at the same pace all through the day.

If you can understand your daily rhythm, then you can arrange things so that the most demanding jobs are dealt with when you are at your peak. The great thing about exercise is that it enables you to "program" your body into a regular routine. The bodily rhythms respond to the regular daily arrangements—that is, sleep, meals and exercise—and if you are forced to make changes in your timetable, the repetition of your daily exercise will enable your body to adjust to the change. When I was competing at a track international we had the usual problems of air travel—time changes and changes of meals. From experience I found that the routine of regular running enabled me to adapt much more quickly to the changes than most travelers. After a flight to New Zealand I found that two days after my arrival my training performances were back to normal. On another occasion I ran for Britain in a match on a Monday afternoon, flew to Jamaica the next day and raced, quite successfully, on the Thursday. If one can adapt quickly enough to meet the demands of competitive racing, then one can certainly adapt quickly to meet the demands of ordinary life.

Applied to the daily exercise program, the concept of rhythm demands that you train at the same time every day. When the body's internal clocks are adjusted to this, the benefits of training will be greater and the ill effects less.

To sum up my four ideas briefly:

1. Most of the body's cells are renewable, and exercise stimulates renewal.
2. The body's natural tendency is to keep itself in optimum working condition.
3. When faced with an overload, the body will respond to meet the extra load.
4. The body has its own internal rhythms, and the understanding of these will help you to know yourself.

I hope that you who read this book are already convinced of the value of exercise in the daily life of civilized man, but I want to tell you one story that I think is significant. When I was in Kenya I ran a coaching course which most of the Olympic team attended. I had a letter from a young Asian named Rustam who was teaching in Kampala and wanted to come to the course. I invited him to come, and he took part in the training sessions, attended the lectures and showed great enthusiasm, though as a runner he had only average ability. That was in May 1972.

Rustam was intending to go to England for a teacher-training course. He already had a place at the college, but as his father was dead he stayed in Uganda one more year while his younger sister was finishing school. It was in August that President Amin ordered all Asians who were not citizens of Uganda to leave the country. Rustam was not worried then because he was a Ugandan citizen, born and bred in the country like his father before him. Then a few weeks later, Amin ordered all Asians to leave the country. Rustam had his college acceptance, so he went to get a British visa. Sorry—no visas were being issued to Ugandan citizens. As the deadline for expulsion of the Asians drew near, he began to feel as if he were in a nightmare. Uganda did not want him because he was Asian; Britain did not want him because he was Ugandan. He had to leave his house, his family business, everything he owned, and go to the airport with a suitcase, destination unknown. Eventually he found himself on a plane to Austria, where in November he was placed, not speaking the language, in a refugee camp.

In the camp, he was in the midst of chaos. At one stroke his home, his wealth and his future had been taken away from him. The only means of identity that he had left was his running, and it was only this, he says, which kept him from complete despair. He managed to retain his self-respect, his identity and his hope for the future, in the face of appalling circumstances in which many others broke down. It might have been the same if he had been a musician or an engineer, but in this case it was his running that gave him the necessary discipline and self-mastery. He is now following a course of studies in Holland, having first learned Dutch (his sixth language), and he is still running.

Of course, few people reading this will ever be faced with such extreme problems, just as few will ever be subjected to the pressures of Olympic competition. However, my point is this: the habit of exercise, which is something natural to the human being, will give you the strength of mind as well as of body to carry you through the emergencies of life, as well as putting the trivialities of the day into perspective. You have only one life, so make the most of it!

5

Philosophy of the Natural Man

Our bodies and our bodily natures are essentially stable, changing slowly. But the world in which we live—that is to say, the human society around us—is not at all stable; it is in a period of population explosion that cannot possibly last. The figures for world population are bandied about in the press so casually and frequently that we come to ignore them. And our complacency is reinforced by the fact that the human race has survived so far: "Something will be worked out." "We have gotten over disasters in the past."

The bald fact is that the human race has never faced the situation that it is in now. The only ways the world population can be kept from doubling every twenty-five years are through widespread disaster, which may be caused by war, disease and famine, or through tight control of resources and birthrates. It is not a pleasant prospect, but there is still hope. If the world population doubles by 2000 and then doubles again by 2050, a figure of fifteen billion is reached. This is considered by some population experts to be a figure at which population could be stabilized, assuming massive efforts to limit the birthrates of the fast-growing countries. This yields an overall figure of three hundred people per square mile of land mass. Even if we make tremendous efforts to populate the barren regions and use the area covered by the sea, there will still be huge population pressures on the inhabitable areas. However, we must remember that Britain has a density of over nine hundred per square mile, has achieved a zero population-growth rate and is capable of being self-supporting for food if necessary; so perhaps we have a slim chance of survival without catastrophe.

The outlook for the next hundred years is not a good one, but it is not totally black. We could produce enough food to feed four times the present population, given enough investment in agriculture and sufficient control of resources, but we shall need a change of attitude as well. We have got to think of the concept of equilibrium—applied to our own regions, to our own countries, to our whole planet. Factors must remain in balance, but when that high population density is reached, as it certainly will be, it will take very little to upset that balance. The effects of overcrowding in a city are to make us more and more interdependent. The city will break down unless the buses run, unless the garbage containers are emptied, unless the food shops are kept supplied, unless the oil supplies are maintained, unless the electricity workers stay on the job: every section of the community has got to understand its responsibility to every other section.

At the same time, the effects of actually living in the city, the stresses of overcrowding, tend to increase aggression and drive people further apart. We have seen quite generally, within the past decade, an increasing polarization of society, an increasing selfishness displayed by different groups of society and a decreasing sense of communal responsibility. The increasing affluence of the past twenty years has not made us noticeably happier or more generous to one another.

The desire for a better standard of living, for a bigger slice of the cake, is a perfectly natural one. It is the natural response of the hunting animal. The outbreaks of frustrated aggression in the streets are perfectly natural too, but that does make them any easier to live with. What we have got to work toward is an understanding of our mutual dependence. The child as he grows must learn where he stands in relation to others—where he stands in relation to his own immediate society and in relation to the whole world, with which he is now inextricably linked.

The need has never been greater for each of us to know reality. Because of this I proffer my own view of what reality is and how we must adjust to it.

Reality lies first of all within our bodies. The growth of cells, the mitotic dance of the chromosomes, the adding of flesh to bone and the pumping of blood down a myriad of corridors. Birth and its pains are reality; so are death and disease, the battles of bacteria and phagocyte and the healing of wounds. We must accept our bodies, come to terms with them, understand them and look after them.

The living world is reality—the decay of leaf into mold, the germination of seeds, worms in the ground, the slow change of the trees. We spring from this, we depend on this and we shall go back to this. We must understand our place in nature. For us as individuals it is a small one, but for us as a race it is all-important. As the dominant species we must, for our own sake, keep the equilibrium.

There are philosophers who argue that nothing is real, that we can know nothing really, because we have only the evidence of our own perceptions. Yet these philosophers continually acknowledge reality by avoiding cars when they cross the street and eating when they are hungry.

Moving away from these concrete realities, what is real in human relationships? The family is real, because we are biologically adjusted to playing roles in the family life. Sex differences and age differences are real, and so are the relationships arising from them. We can understand ourselves only through understanding the roles that we are designed to play. Our needs and our demands will change as we move from one role to another, and if we are ready for this we shall experience fewer internal conflicts.

Arising from the sense of family is the fact that there is no such thing as total freedom. It is an invention of the romantic age, a fantasy of the leisured society. We are not free because we are not isolated.

In understanding our own personalities we must accept the idea of continuous development. If we do not, then we stagnate. Some people remain perpetual adolescents; still more stop developing mentally in their twenties. The industrial society does not concern itself with personal development; people are regarded as work units capable of doing a particular job for forty years. Most young men, after a few trials, become settled into a job, develop to the degree that the job demands of them and then remain at that state of development until they retire. In primitive societies a man's role changed as he grew older. In the precolonial days the children of the Kikuyu of East Africa were divided into age groups every seven years, each age group having its own rights and responsibilities. It was a truly comprehensive system, because promotion to the next rank depended entirely on age. Naturally, within each age group some took a more dominant role than others, but all the men knew that they would eventually achieve the position of elders, who sat in council and made the decisions and the judgments.

The position of authority automatically confers the sense of responsibility and a basic fault of our society is the lack of individual power or responsibility, except within the family circle. Perhaps it is because they have no responsibility in their outside world that people try to free themselves from the family responsibility as well. The wish to achieve total "freedom," or irresponsibility, although very tempting, is in fact a retreat toward infantilism, the nursery world.

The full development of a person requires that he or she accept family responsibilities. Only in this way will society hang together. This does not mean that everyone has to get married; just that we have to accept that we have duties and responsibilities to those around us. No man is an island.

Accepting this, the natural man will move through his natural roles—at first being totally cared for by his family, then as a child learning the tribal customs, the signs, the dress, the rituals, the dances. As an apprentice, student or young warrior he will start to perform useful work, but under guidance and without total responsibility. Then, after the initiation or graduation, he reaches full manhood, has the right to marry and is expected to make his contribution to the society. The next stage is as the father of the family, still making his full contribution, wielding power in the community, responsible for his wife and for his children and their upbringing. Lastly he becomes the elder, the grandfather, making decisions and giving advice to the warriors and workers. With luck he never arrives at Shakespeare's seventh age of man, but if he does become ill or infirm, the community will accept responsibility for him, and for his dependents if they are unable to look after themselves.

We should move through all of these stages, playing out each role to the full, making our productive years as productive as possible but always prepared to move on to the next stage. If we try to play the perpetual student or the great lover after our time has passed, then we only make ourselves ridiculous. However, what the right kind of living can do is extend the active stages—prolong active life, as the pet food is supposed to do, and slow down the aging processes. What is most noticeable about the old people in both Soviet Georgia and the Andes is not the actual chronological age they reach but the kind of life they can lead at the age of ninety.

For ourselves, then, we must prepare for a life of continuous development, using our talents as best we can. To achieve our maximum potential we have to belong to the kind of community in which we can develop fully. We have a choice, nowadays, in the matter of where we are going to belong. Not everyone sees that he has a choice, but we all do. The choice is partly limited, of course, by where we are born, and further limited by our own intelligence and ability, but it is still there. We can be the masters of our own destinies. If we feel strongly enough about it, we can choose the kind of society in which we wish to live.

I am convinced that the tribal unit is the natural one, the one for which our gregarious but competitive natures are best suited. The question is: which tribe are we going to join?

One of the best things about the world today is the freedom of movement we enjoy. Although it is more restricted politically

72

than, say, forty years ago, the economic freedom is far greater. The cost of air travel compared with income gets lower all the time. If you are English-speaking and have some job qualification, a huge slice of the world is open to you still. And even if we do not go overseas, there is a tremendous diversity of life-styles available in our own countries. When I allow myself to be optimistic about the future I see a wealth of different communities, some conventional and some not. Each has its own values and code of behavior. Some are centered around music or theater, some are religious, some are workers' communes or agricultural cooperatives. We already have self-supporting communities within the normal framework of local and national government. With greater regional devolution we could see an increase in communities of like-minded people, running their lives on their own terms and rewarding themselves in their own way.

When I talk about belonging to a tribe, I am serious. Most of us belong to one already, without realizing it. We are born into a tribe that consists of our parents, their relatives and their friends. At first we accept all the values of this group and make friends with those of our own age. As soon as we go to school, however, we meet contemporaries with different backgrounds and different sets of values; the school offers us other choices. The teachers exist as models, for the children's purpose, of different life-styles. Each area of the school has its own ambience, and the children unconsciously opt for certain patterns of life at the expense of others. The choice, however, remains unconscious for most. Teachers always encourage their pupils to cover as wide a range as possible, so as to keep their options open. When the children move on and have to go to work, they encounter other sets of values, which often run counter to those they were taught at school. The world of business has its devotees, and the need to survive forces many to subscribe to its beliefs. They are forced to make compromises, in that they spend time doing things they do not really want to do. At the same time the different worlds that were grouped together at school and sampled in small packets expand and fly apart. The worlds of art, fashion, music, sport, literature and science proclaim their values, exhibit their heroes, demand devotion from their followers. Between family, work and what we may sum up as the leisure world, the individual is pulled in many directions.

To achieve satisfaction you must have a sense of where you belong in all this. You must decide where your allegiances lie. This does not mean that you will cease to lead a normal life in the sense of work and family. It means that you choose consciously what you consider to be important, what kind of achievement matters. Having made this choice, you then find yourself among others of the same view. This is your tribe, and the longer you stay in that group the more you will take on its characteristics.

Of course, very few people will go so far as to join a commune, change their hair and dress style and insist that all the family share their beliefs. For most it is a matter of forming a network of friendships and patterns of activity. Different members of the family can belong to different "tribes" without too much conflict. Even this kind of decision, however, can have a very significant effect on your pattern of life over a long period of time. When E. M. Forster stated that the Wilcox family in *Howards End* belonged to a golf club, he passed over to the reader a whole parcel of judgments on the family and their values. One can have no better example than that book of the "tribal" differences existing within conventional society. These days we see that there are many more tribes, with values that differ even more widely.

Whether membership in your tribe involves you in close contact with the other members depends on the tribe. One may find a group of recreation-vehicle enthusiasts who like to get together for family outings every month, and one may find a group of bibliophiles who in fact never meet in their entire lifetimes, but communicate through letters. What matters is that you have someone else who shares your values and who cares what happens to you. Without this, even the happiest of domestic lives can seem empty. Without a framework your actions seem meaningless; without a path to follow your movements seem pointless.

In the hunter-gatherer days, the maximum size of the tribe was about five hundred people of all ages. Even with modern communications you will find it difficult to keep up worthwhile contact with a greater number than this. If you increase the numbers too much, the contacts are too brief to be meaningful. Within the five hundred there will be fewer than a hundred of your own age group, and it is among these that the small number of close friendships will be formed. It is no longer necessary for the tribe to be in close, continuous contact, but ideally one should have some fellow members within easy talking distance, so that one can discuss day-to-day changes and share experiences.

What I am trying to say is that mere existence is not enough; just surviving and bringing up a family is not enough; mere acquaintanceship is not enough. To live a fully satisfactory life the modern family, like the ancient family, must fit into a relationship with other families; it must belong somewhere. The tribal arrangement, with common heroes, common legends, shared rituals and shared values, provides stability. The children of the tribe grow up knowing where they belong. They can relate to a wider range of people than the immediate family; they can see people of different ages playing different roles. The interdependence of the tribe brings responsibility to the senior members and affords protection to the younger members. This in turn produces tribal loyalty, which binds them closer together.

The tribal system is not all good, however. There are times when the conflict of interests brings two tribes into opposition—one thinks of clashes between hippies and straights, between rival football fans, between motorcycle gangs and seaside residents; but this is avoidable. Violence is less likely to erupt when people have some meaning and purpose in their lives than when they are merely disturbed products of an overcrowded urban environment. The values that give them meaning and purpose may differ wildly, but if they serve to bind people together they are justified—with certain reservations to take into account such tribes as the Mafia and the SS!

Because this book is concerned with our physical nature, I have not so far said anything about belief or purpose. From the physical point of view, anything that gives a person or a tribe a reason for living will enhance its chances of survival. However, I would not be honest if I did not include, however briefly, a personal view of our function on this earth.

I suppose that my views could be summed up in three phrases. From the *Rubaiyat* of Omar Khayyam: "One thing is certain and the rest is lies. The flower that once has blown for ever dies." From Voltaire's *Candide*: "We must dig our garden." From Marcel Proust: "We must all play our parts."

We are present on this earth for a short time. We are part of the planet—the most important part, because we are the controlling part. Our function is to continue the race and preserve the land. Our purpose is to use what talents we have to their fullest ability. Our duties are, first, to achieve a state of harmony between ourselves and the world around us; second, to achieve a positive and harmonious relationship with our immediate family; and third, to achieve a positive relationship to the wider world around us, in whatever sphere we find ourselves in.

How can we achieve these things? To be at peace with ourselves, we must be able to feel that we are physically right, living in the right way and developing our talents. To achieve harmony with those around us we must think carefully about our duties and our responsibilities to our families and our friends. If you are living only for yourself, however successfully, the satisfaction will not be lasting, because we are social animals. We must be part of a continuum, carrying on from one generation to another.

The hardest thing to achieve is a state of contentment in relation to the world around you, even if you are lucky enough to be wildly successful. The world of television and newspapers has created the global village, and in relation to the "success" figures we see there, 99.99 percent of us are bound to be failures. For status we must look to our local community—our own tribe—and forget about the rest. Within our own tribe we must live like the tribe in its territory—building and preserving, not squandering and destroying. If when you come to die, you can say, "I have done something for my tribe; I have advised them well; I have built something for my children which will stand for the future," then you can feel that you have lived properly.

All I am qualified to talk about, however, is the way in which we can adjust our physical nature so that the workings of the mind are helped, not hindered, by the working of the body. When you start on one of my exercise programs, remember that it is meant to be something positive, not negative. It is supposed to add something to your life, not to make you suffer. As much as possible of your exercise should be out of doors, so that you can feel, smell and hear what is going on in the world. You should let the wind blow over you and around you, feel the ground under your feet and see the clouds moving. This is the reality to which you belong. When you feel part of it, it will always comfort you.

6

Exercise—The Natural Way to Health

It should now be clear that the biggest single difference between the natural man and his civilized descendant is in the amount of exercise taken in the natural state. With the knowledge now available to us, it is not hard to work out programs that will make up for this deficiency. The only problems lie in the diversity of activities that are available and in the wide differences between individuals. One cannot recommend a single program that will benefit everyone equally; if I say, "Run twenty minutes a day," it might be physically impossible as well as dangerous for an unfit person, and useless to a really fit one. What we must do is look at the various benefits that we get from exercise and work out the value of different kinds of sporting activities; only then can we plan programs to suit individual needs.

There is no such thing as absolute fitness. Fitness just means "suitability" for a particular task. A man who is fit as a tennis player is not necessarily fit as a swimmer. What we call fitness is a blend of a number of qualities, and when we say that someone is a very fit person we mean that he has developed most of these qualities. Fitness to me means the proper development of seven attributes: muscular strength, endurance, flexibility, body weight, circulatory system, breathing system and stress tolerance.

MUSCULAR STRENGTH

This is the most obvious attribute of the fit person, but in fact one of the least important in terms of fitness for modern life. There are few tasks that require strength in our everyday life, apart from moving the chest of drawers or changing a tire. However, although bulging muscles are not a necessity, the development of proper muscle tone *is*. By muscle tone I mean the state of readiness of the muscle. If your muscle tone is poor, movements cannot be accurately controlled. A muscle with poor tone does not respond quickly to signals; it is not that the message travels slowly down the nerves, but that the actual muscle fibers respond slowly and unevenly. By exercise and practice of particular skills, the muscle is trained to give the maximum response to the signal.

A properly trained muscle system will make a tremendous difference in every aspect of your life. Ordinary walking, standing and sitting use muscles all the time. To maintain your posture, sets of muscles are always at work: for example, when you are standing, the muscles in your back and the muscles of your abdomen are both slightly tensed. Not all the fibers are contracting, only a small fraction of them, while the others are resting. It is as if you had a work force operating on a shift basis. In a slack, untrained muscle, few of the members of the work force are used to work, but in the trained muscle they are all used to it, and so the load is shared and the muscle does not get tired.

Furthermore, we know that the individual fibers become more efficient with training. The amount of energy used by each fiber increases with training; thus you are getting more work out of every pound of muscle. This is why a trained sportsman does not usually have huge muscles, even though the strength of the muscles he uses may have greatly improved.

There are some occasions in life when an increase in pure strength is required. Anyone interested in the power sports— weight lifting, boxing or hammer throwing, for example—or in the speed sports will need to strengthen particular muscle groups. Speed depends mostly on muscle strength: the more fibers there are contracting at any one moment, the more pull is exerted at either end of the muscle and the faster will be the movement. It also depends on relaxation. Muscles always work in opposing pairs. When you bend your arm the biceps muscle, on the inside of the arm, contracts and the triceps muscle, on the outside of the arm, has to stretch. If it is not properly relaxed it will resist the stretching movement and thus slow down the bending of the arm. This becomes very important if you are trying to move quickly. With training, muscles become better adapted to the rapid alternation between contraction and relaxation. This means that the fit muscle is less likely to suffer from a tear or "pull" than the untrained muscle.

Muscular strength, under the influence of the male sex hormones, usually increases rapidly in the adolescent boy, the amount of muscular development being determined genetically. However, tremendous changes can be produced by proper strength training. The strength of a muscle group can be more than doubled, and its endurance increased even more than that.

There is a natural tendency for muscle power to decrease with age as the number of fibers in the muscle gradually diminishes, but use and disuse have a lot to do with this. A man of seventy who has maintained his muscular strength with exercise will be able to outperform a man of thirty who has done nothing in the way of exercise. Everyone who plays a game and is concerned about his performance worries about the loss of speed as he gets older. This "speed" is a combination of the reaction time, which changes little; the readiness of the whole body to respond; and the state of the muscle itself. The loss of the rapid response is partly due to a change of "attitude," in that adrenaline is produced less quickly and the body has to be "worked up" into readiness. We must also remember that strength is related to body weight. Although a trained man of 120 pounds may be stronger than an unfit man of 160 pounds, he will not be stronger than a bigger man who has done the same amount of training.

To sum up, everyone needs all-around muscular tone, but strength, though impressive, is not an essential. The kind of strength programs I have put forward in Chapter 11 will all develop tone and strength, but for specific strength building you will have to go to instructional books on weight training and body building. The value of isometric exercises, circuit training, rowing machines and other aids to fitness is considered in Chapter 11.

ENDURANCE

This is an umbrella word that covers many different meanings in common use. I am using it here in the sense of muscular endurance. The other meanings are covered in the term "stress tolerance."

Endurance is one of the greatest human qualities. It is the only quality, apart from intelligence, in which man surpasses most of the other animals. All the more reason, therefore, that we should cherish it and make the most of it.

Muscular endurance itself has several meanings. For example, if you pick up a brick and hold it at arm's length, it will not be long before your arm gets tired and you have to drop the brick. How long you can hold it depends on the "local muscular endurance" of the muscles of your arm. If you put a rucksack on your back and set off with some friends for a walk over the mountains, you will soon discover a difference in the powers of endurance of your party. Although they are not moving at a fast enough pace to get out of breath and although they are not short of food, some will be tired after an hour's walking and others still fresh after five hours. This is what I call "general endurance." Another aspect of this is seen in the way people respond to a series of hard days of mountain walking, or to playing tennis four times in a week. A man may be very good for one or two days and then fold up completely, whereas another may get better and better as the days go by.

What most people think of as endurance is the ability to keep up the pace in a long-distance race—say, a ten-thousand-meter race. This is only partly due to local and general powers of endurance, and far more due to the efficiency of the heart and lung systems. In the primitive condition man developed all three forms of endurance: the ability to march and fight day after day, the ability to chase the antelope for two hours and the ability to wield spear and shield without tiring. All three types of endurance need to be developed in the civilized man as well, to enable him to get the most out of his life. From my own experience as a runner, I know that the ability to keep going under severe physical pressure has stood me in good stead. Not only does it give you the confidence to throw yourself into any kind of physical activity, but it may save your life in an emergency.

In a situation demanding prolonged physical exertion, the man with endurance is less likely to fumble or to make a wrong decision. He is the first to recover from fatigue and thus the first to adapt to a new situation. You may never find yourself having to walk fifteen miles through a desert or a snowstorm, or survive forty-eight hours on a raft, but the knowledge that you have the stamina to do so eases the stresses of daily life. Coping with crowded streets or heavy housework is much less of a strain for the trained man or woman, and if the car breaks down the thought of a two-mile walk is no problem.

Building up endurance is an essential part of the programs I have listed. One of the comforting factors is that it is not an attribute that diminishes with age. Though absolute speed and strength may fall off in later life, powers of endurance do not. There are many fine examples of this from different sports. One of the greatest endurance feats was performed by Edward Payson Weston, who walked from New York to Los Angeles and back, covering about seven thousand miles, at the age of seventy, in 1918. Larry Lewis, a San Francisco waiter, has become a legend in athletic circles. At the age of one hundred he was still running five miles regularly, and he continued to train until his death at the age of one hundred and four. Equally remarkable was the feat of Mr. Christos Iordanidis, a ninety-five-year-old Greek, who in 1974 completed a marathon (twenty-six miles) in six hours forty-two minutes.

Perhaps more significant to the ordinary man is the way in which the high level of performance, expected from a man in his twenties, can be extended into the forties or even fifties. Anyone who can run the marathon race, whose distance demands great endurance, in under three hours can regard himself as a marathon runner, and anyone who can run it in under two and a half hours is approaching international standard. At the time of writing, one of the fastest marathon men in the world is the forty-one-year-old New Zealander Jack Foster. He ran two hours and eleven minutes to finish second in the British Commonwealth Games of 1974. Perhaps more remarkable still is the Swede Eric Ostbye, who at fifty-two years of age is still one of the best marathon men in his country, running it in about two hours twenty-five minutes. If it is possible to perform at this level at the age of fifty-two, it should be easy for the ordinary man to retain endurance throughout his life.

The exercise programs that I have worked out will help to retain endurance, but the most important factor is your attitude. The man who steps aside from any physical challenge with the excuse that he is "too old for that sort of thing" will soon become too old in reality. Muscles will keep their strength and endurance only if they are used; if they are not used they will start to age more rapidly. By the time you reach your fifties you may have to make some compromises about the kind of sport you engage in or the intensity with which you engage in it, but there are very few sports that cannot be carried on for most of your life.

FLEXIBILITY

This, I think, is one of the weakest links in the human makeup. Walking erect on two legs is not easy. Among all the rest of the mammals we find other means of support. The majority, of course, go on four legs, with the backbone, supported by the two pairs of limbs, providing a strong support from which the main organs hang like washing on a line. When the animal goes on two legs the arms are available for other purposes, such as carrying a spear or using a typewriter, but the additional strain on the backbone and the muscles associated with it is enormous. The stomach and intestines and, in the female, the developing fetus are all supported by the backbone and tend to pull it forward. To compensate for this, the muscles in the lower part of the back, connecting the backbone with the sacrum, have to remain in a state of tension to preserve the upright posture of the spine. Similarly, the neck muscles have to remain in tension to support the head. Lower down, in the legs, the muscles and ligaments supporting the hip and knee joints have to support the whole weight of the body. During movement they have to adapt to sudden changes in the amount and direction of the strain.

It is a common human fault that poor body posture and lack of flexibility lead to muscular troubles in later life, often with a good deal of pain. The body can cope with its own weight, but if the posture is wrong and the muscles are weak then undue strain occurs. If there is a lack of flexibility then a rapid movement is not automatically followed by the necessary adjustments in the supporting muscles. The protein in the ligaments, which give support to the joints, loses its elasticity.

This increasing stiffness is to some extent inevitable, but we can see the differences between those who have made a special effort to keep their flexibility and those who have not. Gymnasts, tumblers, yoga practitioners and dancers who keep up their exercises remain flexible. But the majority of civilized adults suffer increasingly with age from stiff joints, stiff necks, slipped disks and low back pain. Sudden movements, a fall or a slip, become more and more dangerous when the body is inflexible. The ligaments tear instead of stretching, and the stiff person falls more heavily than the flexible.

The thing about inflexibility is that by the time it becomes apparent it is too late to do much about it. Only by regular exercise throughout life will it be avoided. This means that when a man or woman stops taking part in regular sports and games he should go straight onto a program of daily exercise. Remember that life to the natural man and woman was one of ceaseless activity. It may have been drudgery at times, but it did use the body—and the body is designed to be used.

BODY WEIGHT

No aspect of fitness is more discussed than body weight, and the idea that it is a good thing to keep your weight down is now generally accepted. In the most primitive agricultural communities, where most people are on the level of mere existence, being a fat man is regarded as a sign of health. This makes sense when the greatest danger the community faces is that of starvation. The fat man will survive hard times better than the thin man—he can break down his own fat to obtain energy when there is not enough food to eat. This idea about fatness survives still in regard to babies.

A baby is born thin, with very little fat under the skin, but in the first few months of life it becomes very chubby. This is a natural pattern and has a purpose: the fat baby is much better protected against the cold and much better protected against a temporary shortage of food. In the old hunting era there was always the possibility of a few days when food was scarce and everybody went hungry. At such a time the thinner babies were more likely to die through hunger (a baby needs more food in proportion to its body weight, and so babies are far more vulnerable than children or adults). What was originally an effect of selection working through evolution later became a conscious process. It does not take a lot of experience to realize that the baby that puts on weight quickly after birth has a greater chance of surviving its early years. Parents have therefore regarded the fat baby as the healthy baby. This is fine when it is a baby, but it does not hold good when the baby becomes a toddler. The overweight child tends to acquire habits that persist and affect its whole pattern of life.

Body weight depends originally on the person's height and build, but increase in weight is usually caused by increasing amounts of fat. Man is unusual in having a thick layer of fat under the skin. This affords protection against cold, which in other animals is provided by hair, but the reason behind it has not yet been satisfactorily explained. One theory is that at one stage in his evolution man was an aquatic mammal, living in the sea and on the seashore as a means of escape from fiercer animals. This is supported by the way in which the body hairs lie on the skin. There is, however, no fossil evidence supporting this theory. Most zoologists prefer to think that the loss of hair came about as part of our development when we became hunting animals in hot climates, and that the development of fat under the skin came about as a later adaptation to life in colder climates.

In any case, the fat is laid down in cells that are modified for fat storage. It is now established that the child who acquires the "habit" of laying down a lot of fat in early life keeps that habit when it grows up. This is not just a matter of how much it eats and exercises; the fat child actually converts a larger proportion of its food into fat than the thin child. The pattern of how much of the food is burned up for energy and how much is stored as fat is governed by the thyroid gland, which controls the metabolic rate. Different people differ considerably in their metabolic rate; it is an inherited characteristic, but, as we know, it is also affected by the environment. What happens in the cases I have mentioned is that the inherited metabolic pattern may be distorted by the treatment in early life. In poor countries it is distorted by malnutrition; in rich countries, by overfeeding.

Once the pattern of fatness is laid down, it will affect the behavior, the way of life and even the personality of the child. This is followed later by an effect on health. What may often set in is a vicious circle of cause and effect. The fat child is at a disadvantage: the extra fat makes him hot, and the extra weight he has to carry makes him breathless, when he is taking exercise. He therefore has a tendency to avoid exercise, which may lead to avoiding other children so that he is not forced to take part in their games. The fat child who is cut off from his playmates or is actually rejected by them may then eat even more as a compensation for lack of affection. This leads to his getting fatter and exercising even less. The longer the pattern continues, the more firmly does the fate of the fat boy become sealed, and the more certain he is to become a fat man.

Increasing weight in adults is a different story. People whose formative years were affected by the Depression or by the Second World War did not have much chance of overeating. Their food intake was balanced by their exercise; with fewer cars and labor-saving machines they took more exercise anyway. As they passed the age of thirty, their standard of living rose and the amount of time they spent on sport grew less. With more money to spend, and a greater choice of food in the stores to spend it on, they ate more than they had eaten when they were young and so they started to put on weight. These are the people who are now beginning to suffer from the troubles I discussed in Chapter 3.

Control of body weight is the most important way in which exercise can benefit your health. We can work out the sums to show the effects of changing either your intake of food or the amount you use up each day. One ounce of fat when respired by the body releases 267 calories of energy. A pound of fat is therefore equivalent to 4,272 calories. If you play squash for half an hour you will burn up an extra 450 calories in addition to your normal daily usage. The total amount of fat which could be lost as a result of the game of squash is no more than two ounces. It hardly sounds as if it were worth the effort, but there is more to the story than this.

First of all, the effect of two ounces at a time is not insignificant. If you exercise in that way three or four times a week, that is half a pound a week, two pounds in a month. That does not sound like much either, but twenty-five pounds in a year is a different matter entirely. Nor is that all. By exercising in this way regularly you get very hot. This rise in body temperature puts the body into the same situation as that of a man in a hot climate. If the body temperature gets too high, then automatic measures come into effect to lower it. One of these is sweating, and the other, slower but more significant, is a reduction in the thickness of fat under the skin. It is no coincidence that the men living around the Equator are skinny and the Eskimo are chubby. The colder the climate, the thicker the layer of fat. Raise the temperature of your own internal climate and you will lose fat.

We must remember to make a distinction between permanent and temporary weight loss. I was once running in a ten-thousand-meter race at Stade Colombes in Paris. In the changing rooms there was a jockeys' scale on which, just for interest, I checked my weight before and after the race. Although it was on a cool after-noon in October, I lost over two kilos—four and a half pounds—during the twenty-nine minutes of the race. Only a few ounces of this was due to carbohydrate consumption; the rest was water, which was soon put back in the drinking after the match. If I had continued to lose weight at that rate during my run across the United States, I would never have gotten across California; long before I reached Blythe I would have dwindled to fifteen pounds and blown away in the desert wind!

I shall say a bit more about weight in Chapter 7, but the thing to remember is that you may make up the loss of liquid as quickly as you like, but you should not increase the amount you eat.

One of the nice things about using up calories is that it does not matter how fast you work at it, so long as you complete the task. It takes the same number of calories to run a mile in ten minutes as it does to run it in five minutes. So there is always a chance for you, however overweight or out of condition you may be, to achieve what you set out to do. For this purpose you can choose the form of exercise you enjoy most. You can use up more calories playing a round of golf than in playing a game of squash, and the worse a golfer you are the more calories you will expend. The crucial thing is the *number* of miles you move per day. Table 3 gives the approximate calories per minute used in each sport and the amount used up in a game of normal length.

TABLE 3

Sport	Calories per minute	Calories per game
Archery	3–5	200 (variable)
Badminton	6	200–300
Baseball	2–8	variable
Basketball	9	300–400
Bowling	4	150–250
Cross-country running	10–12	300–500
Cycling	7–15	400–900 (1 hour)
Football (all forms)	5–12	500
Golf	4–7	700
Hockey	7–9	500
Horseback riding	3–10	400 (1 hour)
Rowing	7–11	500 (1 hour)
Skiing	5–18	800 (2 hours)
Squash	10–18	500
Swimming	5–15	600 (1 hour)
Tennis	6–8	400 (1 hour)
Walking	3–5	240 (1 hour)

Some sports are impossible to measure in these terms. The "sitting-down" sports like auto racing certainly involve energy expenditure, although the physical work involved is not great. The combined effect of sweating, constant muscular tension and a speeded-up metabolic rate accounts for the loss of weight that a driver experiences during a race.

Even for the sports listed in the table, however, the values can be only approximate. Two men playing the same game may have vastly different rates of energy use. This can be illustrated by an ingenious experiment that was once done on tennis players; they were filmed throughout their game and then the film was run through, with each individual being timed for the periods when he or she was actually moving about on the court. It was found that some fat girls moved about less than half as much as the thinnest girls; thus, although they both spent the same time playing tennis, the fat girls used up only half as many calories.

CIRCULATORY SYSTEM

This comes second only to weight as the fitness factor that most needs working on. The figures on diseases of the heart and the blood system should be sufficient to prove this point. Fortunately, the remedy for these troubles is available to us all.

The circulatory system can be divided into three sections: the heart, the large vessels (arteries and veins) and the tiny vessels that actually supply the cells—the capillaries. They are not dead tubes but made of living cells. The health of these cells and therefore the efficiency of the blood vessels depends on the health of the whole body. When a man puts on extra weight, it has been estimated that a mile of capillaries is needed for each additional pound in weight. This means that a man who is, say, twenty pounds overweight is putting a greatly increased strain on his heart, because the blood has to be pumped that much farther.

The main feature of athletic training is the training of the heart. Say to yourself three times: "Running makes the heart grow stronger." When we take strenuous exercise the heart has to beat faster. If this exercise continues for some minutes the heart itself needs more oxygen, which it takes mainly from the coronary arteries. If by training we keep the heart working hard, the heart responds by developing a richer blood supply to its own muscle cells. This is the vital aspect of training and the reason why those who take exercise continually are less likely to suffer from failure of the coronary supply. In the fit man, the coronary arteries develop many side branches. A blockage in one of the branches will not be fatal, because the other branches can carry enough blood to give the heart the oxygen supply it needs.

Training also has other significant effects. Several research workers have found that exercise has a direct effect in lowering the quantity of triglycerides (fats) and cholesterol in the blood. These are the substances most present in the deposits on artery walls, the deposits that cause them to harden.

An idea that dies hard is the fallacy that the so-called athlete's (enlarged) heart is some sort of pathological condition. In point of fact, the athlete usually *does* have a larger heart, along with three associated benefits: increased pumping capacity, increased heart reserve and the ability to provide more oxygen to the tissues as work increases. Both his resting heart rate and his rate with submaximal effort are considerably lower than those of the non-athlete. This can be proved when someone's pulse rate is taken before he starts a training program and continues to be measured as training proceeds. Over a period of weeks it will be found that the rate of the heartbeat, when the person is completely at rest, gradually decreases. This resting pulse (usually measured immediately after waking up in the morning) will be seventy to eighty beats per minute for the average man or woman, but with training it may well drop to sixty or below. My own resting pulse, when I am really fit, has been as low as thirty-eight. This is because the heart, being stronger than before and capable of pumping more at each beat, does not have to work as hard to keep the body supplied with oxygen. (See Chapter 7.)

The other effect of training is to improve the circulation to the working muscles, with the result that more capillary vessels develop in the muscles that are being used most. Although these capillaries are not in use when you are at rest, in an emergency, when more oxygen is needed, they open up to allow more blood to flow. This means that you can "switch on" to a higher rate of exercise when you really need to. Of course, this would not be any good unless your heart had also strengthened so that it could deal with this extra effort.

BREATHING SYSTEM

The size of your lungs does not have very much to do with your fitness, any more than the size of your head is related to your intelligence. When we are breathing in and out, only one-quarter to one-third of the oxygen available is actually taken from the lungs into the bloodstream. Only in times of great oxygen demand does the efficiency of the breathing system become really crucial. For the ordinary person, an inadequate breathing system may cause slight discomfort during exercise and so discourage him from taking as much exercise as he should.

To start with the simplest things, people ask me, "Is it better to breathe through the mouth or the nose?" The answer is that at rest you should breathe through the nose: the air as it comes in through the nose is warmed and the dust is removed. When you are taking exercise, however, you have to breathe through the mouth in order to get enough air into your lungs. When you are exercising hard you will be breathing through nose and mouth simultaneously, to get as much air in per minute as possible.

In order to fill your lungs properly, you must breathe "from the stomach." Instead of breathing in by raising your chest, you use your stomach muscles to pull down your diaphragm. When you are taking heavy exercise and have to breathe really deeply as well as quickly, the two kinds of breathing movement are combined. The stomach movement is followed by the chest movement, so that the maximum amount of air is taken in, and the chest is consciously contracted to force the air out of the lungs again. When you are used to regular exercise you do not have to think about breathing, because the coordination of muscle movement and breathing becomes automatic. When I am running steadily I complete one in-and-out breathing movement every four strides, but when I am running hard I breathe in and out every two strides.

SMOKING

This seems the logical place to consider the effects of smoking on health. Everyone is now aware of the positive relationship between cigarette smoking and lung cancer. The fact that a few people can smoke heavily and not develop lung cancer does not disprove the relationship. What is less often realized is that smoking is the cause of bronchial diseases and strongly linked with heart disease. Smokers have a higher incidence of heart disease than nonsmokers. The increase in your heart rate, with its corresponding increase in blood pressure, can easily be measured when your pulse is taken before and after you smoke a cigarette.

As far as fitness is concerned, smoking can easily be shown to affect your oxygen-intake ability, and hence your maximum work rate; it does not affect sprinting speed, which depends solely on muscle power. What smoking does do is impede the passage of oxygen through the alveolar membrane into the blood. A controlled experiment found that inhaling cigarette smoke caused an average decrease in airway conductance of thirty-one percent. This may not impede your capacity for normal life, when your oxygen demand is low, but it has a great effect on your work capacity, when you are breathing hard and trying to get as much oxygen in per minute as possible.

Putting these different aspects together, one can say that if you do not inhale the smoke, and if you smoke only a few cigarettes a day—that is, not more than five—this will not prevent you from reaching a satisfactory fitness level. It is once again a matter of individual judgment. I myself enjoy the occasional cigar—only one or two a week—and the marginal effect on my health is offset for me by the pleasure I get.

STRESS TOLERANCE

.I think that the gains from the natural life and the exercise habit are almost as great in this area as in those of body weight and heart fitness. As I discussed in Chapter 3, stress is both necessary and dangerous. The problem is finding the balance. When one reads of the regime in some of the English public schools of the Victorian era, it is no wonder that there was so much ill health among schoolboys of that time, or that some of them grew up seriously imbalanced. Severe pressure will bring out the best only in the few hardy souls; it will stunt the development of many others.

We cannot avoid stress. It is an inevitable part of living. According to the famed stress theory of Dr. Hans Selye, the body is designed to respond to stress. But the stress mechanism may be exhausted by repeated, prolonged, unrelieved stresses.

Yet stress need not go unrelieved. Very probably you have had the experience of being in a stress situation, under pressure, extremely tense, caught up in some problem, worried and anxious about it and finding it difficult to sit still. Your body seemed to cry out for movement. You may have gotten up and paced the room.

Very often, in moments of stress, physical activity can serve as a relief valve. With stress, there is, as we have seen, an outpouring of adrenal-gland hormones intended to ready the body for activity. Some investigators have suggested that without the activity, substances derived from these hormones may accumulate in the heart and over a long period of time affect heart function. With physical activity, such substances may be destroyed and further accumulations may be prevented.

There are several physical disciplines, of which yoga is the chief, that teach you to achieve relaxation from tension and stress. They are all valuable, yet I believe that the same effect is achieved, after a hard day, by a brisk walk, a good jog or run, a well-fought game of tennis or squash—and of course, all of these activities bring heart-lung and weight-loss benefits which static forms of relaxation do not.

SEX

The last of the natural functions that must be considered is sex. The present preoccupation with sex, to the exclusion of many other pleasures, can be likened to monkeys masturbating in a cage. It grows out of boredom. Certainly sex is a pleasure, as is the fulfilling of all our natural functions, and certainly the human is a highly sexed animal, but the obsession with the sex act is not natural. Sex is only one of nature's ways of programming us to play certain roles, and the true fulfillment of your sexual nature lies just as much in the playing out of the roles for which you are biologically designed as it does in the performance of the sex act.

Where does sex come into exercise? It plays its part first of all as a motivator—we work for approval from the opposite sex, and we like to look good. Sex certainly does not rank as good exercise in the sense that it can compare with skipping rope, jogging, etc. During sexual play and orgasm, heart rate and blood pressure do increase, but more in relation to excitement than to exercise.

However, sex is good exercise in that it is more enjoyable than jogging and tends not to become as boring. Just as in sport, active participation is a lot better than spectating, which produces the tensions without the exercise! Considering the effects of sex on active sport, I am sure, from my own experience, that a relaxed and happy sex life is as good for your sport as it is good for your life—it is the natural thing to do.

The subsequent chapters show you the way in which to prepare and carry out the kind of exercise program that is right for you. This will impose a certain amount of stress on your system, but if you have assessed yourself correctly at the beginning, it will never be an intolerable amount. As you improve, you stretch yourself a little more. And it is when you are making that extra bit of effort that it is doing you good. When you have got into the exercise habit, you are getting back to the natural life, and I can promise you that you will feel and look much better for it.

Sleeplessness, digestive troubles, constipation, lethargy after work, accumulating nervous tension—you can work off all these problems by leading a life that includes regular exercise. In order to fulfill its functions, your body must be allowed to do what it is designed to do—to get out into the open air, run, jump, walk and generally be used.

7

Assessing Your Own Fitness

The objectives of this chapter are, first, to help you find out where you stand before starting on an exercise program and, second, to show you how you can keep a check on your fitness as you go along.

The first thing that has to be said is that if you have any history of blood-pressure or heart problems, or if you have suffered from any serious illness within the past six months, you should have a medical checkup before starting exercise. In the above cases there is no reason why you should not be able to start on some form of exercise—indeed, it is recommended for recovery from many forms of heart disease—but you must know your state of health beforehand. Similarly, a checkup is advisable for those who have lived a sedentary life even with no history of illness. For one thing, it would ruin my case for exercise if you dropped dead while doing something overstrenuous.

Your medical checkup should include a blood-pressure test and a cardiac-stress test. If either should produce an abnormal finding, discuss with your doctor the advisability of starting on a graduated program of exercise. If you are over forty and have not had a checkup within the last five years, I would advise you to have one, unless you are already in the habit of regular, fairly strenuous

97

exercise, in which case there is probably nothing wrong with going a bit further.

Having ruled out the possibility of actual medical danger, you must assess your fitness in respect to the categories listed in the previous chapter.

BODY WEIGHT

A healthy person should reach an optimum body weight in his early maturity and maintain this weight during his life, the actual weight depending on his height and his build. The three basic body types are ectomorph, endomorph and mesomorph. There are measurements that define these words, but basically the ectomorph is thin, spindly, with not much of either fat or muscle; the endomorph, stocky and well covered; and the mesomorph, of medium height with a lot of bone and muscle and not much fat. If you are an endomorph, no amount of exercise is going to give you the body weight of an ectomorph of the same height.

The right weight for you is something personal to you, though it may not be the weight you are at present. Compare yourself with Table 4 for your sex, height and age. Now compare your weight now with your weight at, say, twenty-one, or anywhere between

TABLE 4   AVERAGE WEIGHT
(IN INDOOR CLOTHING)

By age groups
MEN

Height	15–16	17–19	20–24	25–29	30–39	40–49	50–59	60–69
5'0"	98	113	122	128	131	134	136	133
1	102	116	125	131	134	137	139	136
2	107	119	128	134	137	140	142	139
3	112	123	132	138	141	144	145	142
4	117	127	136	141	145	148	149	146
5	122	131	139	144	149	152	153	150

Height	15–16	17–19	20–24	25–29	30–39	40–49	50–59	60–69
6	127	135	142	148	153	156	157	154
7	132	139	145	151	157	161	162	159
8	137	143	149	155	161	165	166	163
9	142	147	153	159	165	169	170	168
10	146	151	157	163	170	174	175	173
11	150	155	161	167	174	178	180	178
6′0″	154	160	166	172	179	183	185	183
1	159	164	170	177	183	187	189	188
2	164	168	174	182	188	192	194	193
3	169	172	178	186	193	197	199	198
4	—	176	181	190	199	203	205	204

WOMEN

Height	15–16	17–19	20–24	25–29	30–39	40–49	50–59	60–69
4′10″	97	99	102	107	115	122	125	127
11	100	102	105	110	117	124	127	129
5′0″	103	105	108	113	120	127	130	131
1	107	109	112	116	123	130	133	134
2	111	113	115	119	126	133	136	137
3	114	116	118	122	129	136	140	141
4	117	120	121	125	132	140	144	145
5	121	124	125	129	135	143	148	149
6	125	127	129	133	139	147	152	153
7	128	130	132	136	142	151	156	157
8	132	134	136	140	146	155	160	161
9	136	138	140	144	150	159	164	165
10	—	142	144	148	154	164	169	—
11	—	147	149	153	159	169	174	—
6′0″	—	152	154	158	164	174	180	—

(Source: Build and Blood Pressure Study 1959)

eighteen and twenty-five when you knew it accurately. If you are more than five pounds overweight on either of those comparisons, then you have cause to worry. Other good guides to this weight problem are your waist measurement (has it increased more than an inch since the age of twenty-one?), the sideways view of yourself in a mirror and your skin fold, which shows the amount of fat stored under your skin. This is scientifically measured with calipers at a number of different places, but a pinch between finger and thumb of the skin of your midriff will give you a good idea. If you take a pinch just above your belly button, it should not be more than half an inch thick. If it is more than this, then either you are an Eskimo or else you have got too much stored fat. This, of course, is an arbitrary figure; you could call it a Rule of Tum.

MUSCULAR STRENGTH

Being deficient in this quality, I personally do not rate it very highly! However, if you cannot lift half your own body weight overhead (70 pounds for a 140-pound man), and if you cannot manage six push-ups in succession or three two-handed pull-ups to a beam, then you are weak. This may not matter much in a push-button age, but you will find it difficult to change the tire next time you have a puncture on a lonely road. If you want to stop people from kicking sand in your face, try the strength and weight training exercises. A lack of "local muscular endurance"—see Chapter 6—is revealed by the inability to go on repeating a light but repetitive exercise like raking the lawn or swinging a golf club.

ENDURANCE

See also The Hundred Steps. This is very much a subjective matter, and so you must judge yourself. Can you go through a fully stretched day, either mental or physical, and feel completely recovered the next morning? Can you still engage in the kind of sports and walks that you could in your twenties? How long can you keep on dancing at a party (granted that your interest is sustained)? Endurance has nothing to do with your tolerance of alcohol, which is quite another factor.

HEART AND LUNG FITNESS

The state of fitness of your circulatory system is all-important—see Chapter 6. The simplest guide to this is your pulse rate, at rest and during exercise. Your pulse at rest, lying down or sitting quietly, should be in the range of sixty to eighty beats a minute for men, sixty-five to eighty-five for women. This is the rate your heart has to maintain to supply your body's needs when you are at rest. If you take exercise, the heart has to beat faster, and if your oxygen intake system (your heart, lungs and blood vessels) is rather inefficient, your heartbeat will go up very quickly for even a small amount of exercise. This means in practice that you will get out of breath and tired very quickly.

The simplest ways of measuring your "heart fitness" are by step-testing for a measured time or by running for a measured time or distance. The former is preferred for untrained people; running tests I will discuss later.

The Harvard Step Test has been done on tens of thousands of people over the past fifty years. It is reliable as a measure of your "heart fitness," though it will not predict who is going to win a race. It can be done easily, without elaborate equipment. The only care required is in counting the pulse rate accurately, and it is ad- ·visable to practice taking your pulse to get a good idea of your normal pulse rate, both when you are at rest and when you are standing.

The test itself consists of stepping on and off a bench or chair, twenty inches high, at a rate of thirty steps a minute, each step up or down taking one second. Again it is advisable to practice the rhythm of stepping beforehand—it makes the test more reliable. You will need someone else to help you count the rhythm of stepping and keep you at the right speed. Once you start, the stepping must go on continuously, either for five minutes or until you feel uncomfortably tired, whichever is the shorter. When you feel tired, sit down and rest; after you stop you are allowed a minute's rest before your pulse is taken.

The important thing is your pulse count during the thirty seconds after your minute's rest. This thirty-second count can then be used, together with the length of time you spent in stepping, to give you a Harvard Step Test Score from Table 5.

To sum up, the procedure should be as follows:

1. Find your pulse and measure it for 30 seconds at rest.
2. Practice the "up and down" stepping rhythm, at one step per 2 seconds, for 20 or 30 seconds, then pause to get your breath back.
3. Step at thirty steps a minute for 5 minutes or until you feel tired. Note the length of time you manage.
4. Sit down and rest for 60 seconds after your stepping, then measure your pulse rate for a further 30 seconds.
5. Read off your score. For example, if you stepped for 1 minute 45 seconds, and your pulse count was 55 in the measured half-minute, your score would be 34. If you stepped for 3½ minutes and your pulse was 55 in the measured half-minute, your score would be 62.

What do these scores mean? They are only arbitrary figures, which give relative values, but I would say that any man over thirty who scored 100 or more could consider himself reasonably fit, and any man under forty-five who scored less than 45 would be rather unfit. For women I would suggest figures of 80 and 30. Those who fall between the two values, though not in desperate straits, could be a lot fitter.

TABLE 5 SCORING FOR THE HARVARD STEP TEST*

Total heartbeats 1 to 1½ minutes in recovery

Duration of effort (minutes)	40–44	45–49	50–54	55–59	60–64	65–69	70–74	75–79	80–84	85–89	90–94	95–99
						Score (arbitrary units)						
0 – ½	6	6	5	5	4	4	4	4	3	3	3	3
½ –1	19	17	16	14	13	12	11	11	10	9	9	8
1 –1½	32	29	26	24	22	20	19	18	17	16	15	14
1½–2	45	41	38	34	31	29	27	25	23	22	21	20
2 –2½	58	52	47	43	40	36	34	32	30	28	27	25
2½–3	71	64	58	53	48	45	42	39	37	34	33	31
3 –3½	84	75	68	62	57	53	49	46	43	41	39	37
3½–4	97	87	79	72	66	61	57	53	50	47	45	42
4 –4½	110	98	89	82	75	70	65	61	57	54	51	48
4½–5	123	110	100	91	84	77	72	68	63	60	57	54
5	129	116	105	96	88	82	76	71	67	63	60	56

* From *Physiological Measurements of Metabolic Function in Man* by C. F. Conzolazio, R. E. Johnson and L. J. Pecora, 1963. Used by permission of McGraw-Hill Book Company.

RUNNING TEST

Your ability to cover a certain distance in a certain time will depend partly on your oxygen intake ability (this is what I mean by "heart fitness") and partly on how hard you exert yourself. Someone who is very highly motivated may run himself into exhaustion to cover a mile in, say, six minutes, while somebody else, equally fit, may run the mile in seven minutes with only mild discomfort. However, if we run a fairly long distance at a steady pace the "motivation" factor will not have very much importance. Time over a short distance, such as one hundred or two hundred yards, just indicates sprinting speed, not heart fitness.

What I want you to do in the first test is cover one mile,

NATURAL FITNESS

preferably on a standard outdoor running track (four laps), at as fast a pace as you can comfortably maintain. You should not sprint in at the finish, but keep going at the steady pace, at which your oxygen intake equals your oxygen use. If you cannot run all the way, walk, but keep going. Now check your performance against Table 6. (These tables are designed for ordinary men and women, not for athletes.)

TABLE 6   STANDARD TIMES FOR MILE RUNS (MINUTES)

MEN

Standard	Age 30–37	38–45	46–53	53+
very poor	*>9.15	>10.00	>11.00	>12.00
poor	9.15–8.11	10.00–8.41	11.00–9.31	12.00–10.16
fair	8.10–7.00	8.40–7.11	9.30–8.11	10.15–8.46
good	6.59–6.20	7.10–6.45	8.10–7.20	8.45–8.00
very good	**<6.20	<6.45	<7.20	<8.00

WOMEN

Standard	Age 30–37	38–45	46–53	53+
very poor	>11.00	>11.30	>12.30	>14.30
poor	11.00–9.31	11.30–10.01	12.30–10.31	14.30–11.01
fair	9.30–7.51	10.00–8.01	10.30–8.26	11.00–9.16
good	7.50–7.00	8.00–7.15	8.25–7.45	9.15–8.20
very good	<7.00	<7.15	<7.45	<8.20

* Greater than.
** Less than.

This test should tie up pretty closely with your performance on the Harvard Step Test. It can be used as a method of testing your fitness at any time during your training program.

104

FLEXIBILITY

Although physical-education experts have worked out standard tests for flexibility, they are not easily done on your own, and so we must rely on your judgment. Can you touch your toes without bending your legs? Can you kick your foot above your shoulder height? Can you sit comfortably in a cross-legged position, without a backrest? When lying on your back, can you bring your feet over your head so that they touch the ground behind you? Do you move easily when getting out of the bath or getting up from a low chair? If you can answer yes to all of these, you are not doing too badly, but in "civilized" countries there are very few people over forty, myself included, who could not benefit from improving their flexibility.

THE HUNDRED STEPS

This is a far more demanding assessment of your fitness, but I assume that anyone who has the interest to buy or read this book will not shrink from trying at least a few steps along the way. It tests heart and lung fitness, in the speed that you can comfortably manage, and endurance, both in the general sense and the local endurance of stomach, leg and back muscles, all of which are needed in running. It does not test muscular strength or sprinting speed, but tests the strength of your will, because you will not get many steps along the way unless you have a bit of willpower as well as basic fitness.

For the start, every healthy man and woman under sixty, wearing the right kind of clothing and footwear, should be able to cover a level mile in twenty minutes or less. This puts everybody at Step 1. At the upper level there are thousands of long-distance athletes who can run ten miles in an hour, including some over-fifties and hundreds of over-forties. The majority of these are not

105

TABLE 7   ONE HUNDRED STEPS
TO SUPERFITNESS

STEP	DISTANCE (miles)	TIME (minutes)	STEP	DISTANCE (miles)	TIME (minutes)
1	walk 1	20	37	trot 2	15
2	walk 1	18	38	trot 3	22
3	walk 1	15	39	trot 4	35
4	walk 2	40	40	trot 4	33
5	walk 2	35	41	run 2	14
6	walk-trot 1	12	42	run 4	31
7	walk 2	30	43	trot 5	45
8	walk-trot 1	10	44	run 3	21
9	walk 3	45	45	run 4	30
10	walk-trot 1½	18	46	run 4	29
11	walk-trot 1½	16	47	run 5	40
12	walk 4	60	48	run 4	28
13	trot-walk 1½	15	49	run 5	38
14	trot 1½	14	50	run 3	20
15	walk-trot 4	55	51	run 5	36
16	trot-walk 2	22	52	run 5	35
17	trot-walk 2	20	53	trot 6	45
18	walk-trot 4	50	54	run 4	27
19	trot 2	19	55	run 5	34
20	trot 1½	13	56	run 3	19
21	trot-walk 4	45	57	run 4	26
22	trot 1½	12	58	run 5	33
23	trot 3	32	59	run 6	44
24	trot 2	18	60	run 6	43
25	walk-trot 5	60	61	run 6	42
26	trot 2	17	62	run 4	25
27	trot 2	16	63	run 6	41
28	trot 3	30	64	run 6	40
29	trot-walk 4	42	65	run 5	32
30	trot 2½	20	66	trot 8	60
31	trot 3	27	67	run 6	39
32	trot 3	25	68	run 7	49
33	trot 4	39	69	run 6	38
34	trot 3	24	70	run 7	48
35	trot 5	50	71	run 3	18
36	trot 3	23	72	run 7	47

STEP	DISTANCE (miles)	TIME (minutes)	STEP	DISTANCE (miles)	TIME (minutes)
73	run 7	46	87	run 8	50
74	run 6	37	88	run 9	58
75	run 10	75	89	run 6	36
76	run 7	45	90	run 9	57
77	run 7	44	91	run 10	65
78	run 8	54	92	run 9	56
79	run 8	53	93	run 9½	60
80	run 4	24	94	run 8	48
81	run 8	52	95	run 9	55
82	run 8	51	96	run 5	29
83	run 5	30	97	run 9	54
84	run 9	60	98	run 6	35
85	run 10	70	99	run 9	53
86	run 9	59	100	run 10	60

particularly gifted men, but merely people who like to run and are prepared to work at it. There are even some women who can run ten miles in an hour. Women's marathon running is now an accepted sport in the United States and in some European countries, and the best of the women competitors, including some in their late thirties, can run the twenty-six miles in under three hours.

To get back to the Hundred Steps, how far is an acceptable level? Let me point out first of all that the steps are meant to be a series of tests, and although they are arranged in sequence, some are more easily achieved than others. By training for and achieving one after another you can move from the possible to the impossible. In the earlier stages, some steps test speed and some test stamina. For example, it may be quite easy for a man in his forties to a walk four miles in an hour (Step 12), but quite hard for him to cover one and a half miles in sixteen minutes (Step 11). It is the speeding up that is important, because to do this you have to improve your "heart fitness." The longer sessions (Steps 15, 18, 25) will accustom you to spending a longer time on your feet. You must be confident of your ability to cover five or six miles slowly before you try to do it at a running or jogging pace.

Now that I've said that, the standards that I would set for nonathletes are as follows:

TABLE 8

Standard	Age up to 35	36–39	50–59	60+
	STEP	STEP	STEP	STEP
Acceptable	17	13	10	9
Creditable	23	20	15	12
Good	29	25	21	15

For standards for the athlete or the fit man, see Plan 3 (page 136) in Chapter 9. I am afraid that there are not enough figures from performances by nonathletic women to lay down standards, but I would expect them to be able to get within three or four steps of the men in each age group.

If you get past the "good" stage for your age group, it is up to you how far you wish to go on. I hope that you will use the Hundred Steps in Table 7 as a challenge and as a ladder to greater fitness and greater enjoyment of life.

If you have gone through this self-assessment chapter carefully, you should have a good idea of where you stand; before you go on to the next chapter, check yourself against the following questions:

1. Are you over thirty-five? Add 1 for every seven years over.
2. Do you have a glass of something alcoholic almost every day?
3. Do you smoke more than five cigarettes a day?
4. Is your pulse, when at rest, over 75 (85 for women)?
5. Are you over the "desirable weight" for your age and build? Add 1 for every seven pounds over.
6. Do you take part in less than one hour's active sport per week?
7. Do you walk less than a mile a day during the working week?

8. Take a roll of skin just above your belly button. Is it more than half an inch thick?

If you answer yes to six or more questions, start on Plan 1; if you have three to five yes points, go on to Plan 2, and if two or less, Plan 3.

8

Making a Fitness Plan

Although you will find three samples of training programs for different fitness levels in the next chapter, I cannot possibly be dogmatic about what is the best thing for everybody. It would be dishonest to try. What I am trying to do in this book is awaken you to the need to take exercise and live in the right way, and then show you how it can be done. The question "How much ought I to do?" will not always have the same answer. It depends on what you want to achieve. Do you just want to halt the deterioration and keep fit enough to cope with normal life, or do you want to move into a "plus" state where you can operate on a higher plane altogether? Or would you just like to take a little bit more exercise, eat a little bit less and feel a little bit fitter? You make your effort and you take your choice.

The first thing to decide is how much time you are prepared to spend per week in looking after yourself. I suggest that you need a minimum of one hour a week, split into three or four sessions, to maintain a slightly improved physical condition. If you are prepared to spend two hours a week you can reach quite a high standard, as you can see from the schedules. But there is more to it than just doing the training; once you have decided to do something about your physical state you are going to affect your whole life. If you are taking exercise you are going to sleep better and relax more. You are more likely to eat regular meals containing the right kinds of food. And if you are testing yourself every now and again by one of the assessment methods I have described, there are going to be some days when you will cut out the drinks and get to bed a bit earlier. I am not trying to make you into a fanatic—just trying to make you aware of yourself.

If you have decided to devote one hour a week to exercise, that means a couple of fifteen-minute sessions during the week plus half an hour at the weekend, or fifteen minutes on four days of the week. Those minutes are actual minutes of exercise, with no corners cut. In ten minutes you can do a complete set of flexibility and strength exercises; with five minutes of "heart training" as well, you will soon feel the benefit.

It is very important that you fit your exercise program into some portion of your routine from which it will not easily be dislodged. It is for this reason that so many people take their exercise before breakfast, because they are less likely to be interrupted then than at any other time. Personally I find it extremely difficult to do anything really energetic before breakfast, and prefer to go out for my run in the evening, before supper, if I have been working indoors all day. I find it relaxes me. Try, if you can, to arrange to take your exercise with somebody else once a week or more; you are less likely to forget it. Fix a regular time, during the week and at weekends, giving yourself time to shower and change afterward, and then stick to your plan. It may seem selfish at times, but you are more likely to be of use to other people if you yourself are in a good physical and mental state.

How should you spend this exercise time? If you are under thirty and taking part in a regular sport, then speed, strength and skill are probably what you are looking for. You must choose a program that fits the needs for your particular sport, based on the principles given in Chapter 6. If you are over thirty and hoping to stay fit enough to take part in a variety of activities, then you need a balanced program, of the kind given in Plans 1 and 2 in the next chapter. The older you get, the more you must maintain your flexibility. For your health's sake you must maintain your heart-lung fitness and your endurance, and for the sake of your pride and the occasional game you will want to maintain your muscular strength. By the time you are over fifty you will probably be concerned mostly with flexibility and heart fitness, since your daily program of work and leisure is less likely to demand a great deal of strength or endurance.

Having said that, let me affirm my own belief, backed up by the authority of Dr. Griffiths Pugh, one of England's leading exercise physiologists, that you are never too old to go on doing the things you enjoy doing, so long as you go on doing them. There are men in their seventies climbing mountains and playing tennis; men in their eighties orienteering and playing golf, men in their nineties lawn bowling, running and even, according to some anthropologists, fathering children. You will not, however, find any septuagenarians playing ice hockey and football, or any other "contact" sports. This brings us to the question of evaluating different sports and pastimes from the fitness angle.

In Chapter 6 I compared different sports in terms of calorie expenditure. A look back to the table there (page 89) will enable you to see how many calories you expend in a game of squash or an hour's walking. Obviously, the more energetic the sport, the more calories per hour you are going to burn up, and the longer you go on doing it the more food will be burned up for energy and the less will be turned into fat.

Some sports, however, are positively harmful from the health angle. All the motorized sports—auto racing, rally driving, power-boat racing—tend to increase tension and raise the blood pressure without providing the necessary release in physical exercise. They will bring benefits in terms of strength to certain muscle groups (particularly the upper body), but on the whole they are not health-building. On the other hand, they can obviously be tremendously fulfilling sports, because they present a challenge that is both competitive and dangerous—something that will appeal to the primitive hunting and fighting instincts within us. The very experience of having to make quick decisions in a state of stress is a beneficial one.

Motor sports share with football, boxing, hockey and other contact sports the feature of being physically dangerous. Of course, it is this risk, so like that encountered by the warrior, which gives these sports their "manly" image, but from the strictly medical angle they cannot really be recommended to the middle-aged sportsman. On the other hand, I feel that any sport is better than none, and a man who takes part in his weekly game of basketball—and trains for it—stands a better chance of survival than the crossword-puzzle addict.

If you take part in a weekly contact sport or motor sport and don't train for it, you are asking for trouble. The thing that is really likely to cause damage is a sudden and violent strain imposed on an unprepared body, which is just what the unprepared weekly sportsman is going to encounter. He may get away with it when he is young, but when he reaches, say, his mid-thirties, he may be forced by family or work pressures to miss one or two games. If he then hurls himself into the fray, without any training and quite possibly without any warming up, he is likely to injure himself. What bad luck, you might think—but in fact it is stupidity.

The logical thing for the man who takes part in motor sports or contact sports is training, particularly for the muscles he is going to use most. One of the most impressive performances I have ever seen was that of Jackie Stewart in the first Superstars competition. His performance in a whole range of strenuous sports showed the effects of the training he put in to keep himself fit for auto racing. This is in contrast to the fitness attitudes of many professional athletes such as baseball players, who are extremely reluctant to do anything except practice their ball skills. The people at the very top are always those who appreciate that their skill will be of use only so long as they maintain their bodies properly; but what kind of training these professional athletes ought to do is outside the scope of this book.

NATURAL FITNESS

The ideal sport would be one that involves almost continuous exercise, for calorie consumption and heart training, at a level that would be suitable for a wide age range. Ideally it would be a competitive sport, where people would be able to compete within their own age/sex group, to provide the stimulus to make an effort. This ideal sport should involve as many muscle groups as possible and as wide a range of movement as possible, providing health gains in strength and flexibility. It should also be cheap and easily available to large numbers of the community.

I don't think that such an ideal sport exists, but ski orienteering in Scandinavia probably comes the closest to it. Cross-country running or skiing, orienteering and hill walking all have the advantages of not requiring expensive facilities and of being geared to the individual's own ability level, but not everyone has the countryside on his doorstep. Rowing and swimming probably use more muscle groups than other sports, and the former also scores high for effort level, but it is expensive. Squash, badminton and handball score high for effort level and range of movement, but are rather limiting in use of space—only two people on a court at a time. Team games, such as soccer, hockey, basketball and volleyball, involve more people at a time, but the effort level is not so great.

Table 9 categorizes various major sports and games in terms of effort level. The Level A sports are the most demanding on the heart and lungs, because they need the highest oxygen intake per minute—they are mostly continuous sports, in which the individual is on the go without a break. Some of the Level B sports could come into the Level A category when done at the highest level—championship squash, for example. Because the Level A sports are the most demanding, they are also the ones that will do you the most good, in terms of heart training and caloric consumption; but of course you must be fit for them first.

In preparing my fitness plans I have calculated that fifteen minutes of Level A is worth thirty minutes of Level B, forty-five minutes of Level C or ninety minutes of Level D. Thus you can get your "heart training" effect, and use as many calories, by doing

TABLE 9

Level A sports

Competitive rowing
Cross-country skiing

Running (over 8 mph)
Swimming (crawl or butterfly)

Level B sports

Circuit training (see Chapter 11)
Cycling (over 15 mph)
Handball
Jogging (6–8 mph)

Skipping rope
Squash
Swimming (backstroke or breast-stroke)

Level C sports

Badminton
Basketball
Cycling (10–15 mph)
Football (all forms)
Hill walking
Horseback riding
Rock-and-roll dancing

Skiing (using lift)
Surfing
Swimming (recreational)
Table tennis
Tennis
Trotting (5–6 mph)
Volleyball

Level D sports

Lawn bowling
Baseball
Croquet
Dancing

Golf
Sailing
Walking

an hour's badminton or going for a two-mile run in under fifteen minutes. This categorization is, necessarily, extremely rough, but it will help you to see the pattern of your progress toward fitness.

To construct a balanced fitness program for yourself, you will need to start off with a small amount of "heart fitness" training per week, gradually increasing the amount to the point where you feel you cannot afford to spend more time on it. You should also build up your endurance by including something that keeps you on your feet for a couple of hours once a week or at least once every two weeks.

Some activities are not included here either because their heart-training value is low or because it is hard to assess. Three of these activities—yoga, gymnastics and judo—are the three most valuable ways of increasing your flexibility. To build up your strength, exercises, weight training, circuit training, isometrics and the use of apparatus (see below) are needed, and I have included a short section on weight and circuit training in Chapter 11.

Yoga is dealt with at length in many other books. Apart from its religious connotations, it is an excellent system of self-discipline, which is first-class for improving your flexibility and muscular tone. It is effective in achieving relaxation, lowering tension and maintaining a "normal" blood pressure. Where it is unsound as a means of achieving fitness is in being too static; it has little value as cardiovascular (heart-fitness) training. However, there is no reason why one should not include both yoga sessions and cardiovascular sessions in a week's training.

My own predilection is toward running training as the basis of building fitness. Running forms a basic part of the training for such diverse sports as rowing, boxing, tennis and football. It is a natural activity, cheap, easily accessible and easily geared to the individual's needs. Two popular programs in the United States, jogging and aerobics, have brought increased fitness to thousands of ordinary people. The situation in Britain is slightly different. The British are less a nation of spectators, with every village, town and suburb possessing its infrastructure of sports clubs, where people are already taking some active part in sports. What they need is simple fitness programs to augment the weekly sports, so that people can get more out of them over a longer period.

The fitness plans in the next chapter use a graduated running program, with the proviso that other sports may be substituted. The running itself need not be just straight plodding along the road; indeed, it will be more effective if it is not. In order of intensity, we have jogging (6–8 mph, or 7–10 minutes per mile); straight running (over 8 mph, or faster than 7½ minutes a mile), on either road, track or grass or cross-country; Fartlek running; interval training; repetition training and resistance running (see Chapter 10). All of these are used by serious runners with national ambitions.

Once you have acquired the endurance and fitness to run two or three miles, you can vary the steady pace by putting in short bursts at a faster pace. This is Fartlek. Interval training, the basis of most modern athletics training, consists of running a measured stretch at a fast pace, resting until almost recovered and then running the same distance again. The training effort must be long and hard enough to raise your pulse rate to over 150, and during the interval it should be allowed to fall only to the 100–120 range. Athletes normally run fast bursts of between 200 and 800 meters, with a recovery interval of one to three minutes; this is hard work, but very good cardiovascular training. Repetition running is a more strenuous version of this, with the distances run fast being anything from half a mile to a mile and a half, with long rest periods in between.

Repetition running is probably too hard to interest the "keep-fit" man, but resistance running is the kind of training that can be done anywhere; the running is made harder by being done against resistance of some kind—through sand, up hills, across plowed fields or while wearing heavy boots or a weighted jacket. It is particularly good in strengthening the leg muscles and in building endurance. The cardiovascular benefits are no better than those of interval running or Fartlek, but the psychological benefits, through the strengthening of willpower, are considerable. For more details you should consult a specialized book on running training such as the Bowerman-Harris *Jogging* (Grosset & Dunlap).

Before you go on to look at my sample training schedules, let me summarize the points you should consider in making your own program.

1. Decide what your aims are.
2. Decide how much time you can invest per week.
3. Make a plan for the first four weeks, trying to include training for flexibility, heart training and endurance training, plus whatever you need for your own sport.
4. Start with a weekly load that you can handle comfortably and progress gradually. Don't try to go too fast.

117

5. Do not get stuck in a rut. Use some method of measuring your progress, or have some target to aim for. When you reach your target, aim for a new one.

6. Revise your program every three months.

In Chapter 11 you will find sections on the various forms of indoor training. This will enable you to modify your training program according to the seasons.

9

Graduated Fitness Programs

PLAN 1   BEGINNERS

This plan is arranged in a carefully graduated series of steps, over a twelve-week period, with a step up in the level of training about every two weeks. It is important that those who are not used to taking regular exercise not try to cut corners: it is vital that you be able to cope with each level of training before going on to the next. Do not be ashamed to repeat a week before going on, if you feel that you need it. It does not matter whether you take twelve or twenty weeks to get to the top level of the plan; it is much better to take it slowly and get there, rather than go at it too fast and fail through injuring yourself.

Remember that the plan is just a plan, not a set of commands. The idea is to exercise three or four times a week, starting with something that is quite possible and working up to something that is quite hard. If you are happy to stop at that level, you can do so by using the "maintenance" schedules, but if you are fired with ambition to go on to greater things, you can progress to the standard and then the advanced plan.

The plan is arranged in weekly units, and the exercise may be taken on any of the days in the week; more benefit will be gained, however, if each day's exercise is followed by a day's rest. Therefore a Tuesday, Thursday, Saturday exercise pattern is better than a Wednesday, Saturday, Sunday pattern. This may not matter very much in the easy stages, but will make a difference if you go on to something harder.

WEEK 1
Exercise three times a week. Level D only.

DAY 1: 1-mile walk, without hurrying but without stopping. Once through flexibility exercises (5 minutes; see Chapter 11) without extending yourself.

DAY 2: 1-mile walk, starting easily and stepping out in the second half. Flexibility exercises as before.

DAY 3: 1-mile walk at a brisk pace throughout. Keep your head up and breathe steadily and deeply while walking; 5 minutes of flexibility exercises, counting the number of repetitions of each exercise and doing each one properly.

ALTERNATIVES: 15–20 minutes active of any Level D exercise.

WEEK 2
Exercise three times a week. Level D only.

DAY 1: 1–1½-mile walk, taking it easy. If you have sore feet or any blisters, treat the sore areas and adjust the thickness of your socks to prevent slipping; 6–8 minutes of flexibility exercises, doing the minimum number for each exercise.

DAY 2: 1½ miles continuous walking. Flexibility exercises as Day 1.

DAY 3: 1-mile brisk walk. Flexibility exercises as Day 1. Try to time yourself over a known mile distance. If you can walk it within 18 minutes comfortably (Step 2 in Table 7, page 106), go on to Week 3. If not repeat Week 2.

ALTERNATIVES: 20 minutes active of any Level D exercise.

WEEK 3

Exercise three or four times a week. Level D only.

DAY 1: 1½-mile brisk walk. 6–8 minutes of flexibility exercises, doing one more than the minimum number of repetitions of each.

DAY 2: 2-mile walk, taking it easy. Flexibility exercises as Day 1.

DAY 3: 1-mile brisk walk. Aim at 15 minutes (Step 3 in Table 7). Flexibility exercises as Day 1.

DAY 4: Repeat Day 1.

ALTERNATIVES: 30 minutes *active* of any Level D exercise.

WEEK 4

Exercise three or four times a week. Level D only.

By the end of this week you should have finished the preparatory phase of the schedule and be fit enough for something a little more strenuous. If you suffer from any aches or pains in these first four weeks, do not move on unless you have fully recovered by the end of the week. Instead, consult Chapter 11, take the appropriate measures and repeat the week.

DAY 1: Walk 2 miles steadily; aim at 40 minutes (Step 4 in Table 7). 6–8 minutes of flexibility exercises, including two more than the minimum number of repetitions of each.

DAY 2: 1-mile fast walk. Step out, keeping your head up, and breathe deeply. Aim at under 14 minutes. Flexibility exercises as Day 1.

DAY 3: An hour's walk, taking it easy but not stopping. This is your first endurance challenge of any kind. Try to find somewhere interesting to do it. Do not worry too much about the distance covered, but it should be about 3 miles. Flexibility exercises as Day 1.

DAY 4: As Day 1. Aim at 37–38 minutes for your 2 miles.

ALTERNATIVES: 30 minutes *active* of any Level D exercise.

WEEK 5

Exercise three or four times a week. Level C or D.

DAY 1: Walk for a quarter of a mile, then break into a gentle trot and continue for half a mile. If you feel uncomfortable, walk for 50 yards, then start trotting again. The trotting pace should be very little faster than your brisk walking pace. Walk the last quarter of a mile of your mile course.

DAY 2: 6–8 minutes of flexibility exercises, doing two *below* the maximum number for each, plus one set of the basic three strength exercises. Take these slowly, resting where necessary and doing the minimum number of each.

DAY 3: 40 minutes of steady walking, stretching out any stiff muscles. Flexibility exercises as Day 2.

DAY 4: 2 miles brisk walk. Aim at 35 minutes (Step 5 in Table 7). Flexibility and strength exercises as Day 2.

ALTERNATIVES: 40 minutes *active* of any Level D exercise on Day 3.

WEEK 6

Exercise three or four times a week. Level C or D.

DAY 1: 1 mile of walking and trotting, using short periods of walking to get your breath back. 6–8 minutes of flexibility exercises, doing two below the maximum number for each. 3 minutes of basic three strength exercises, doing minimum number of each.

DAY 2: 35 minutes brisk walking or other Level D activity. Flexibility and strength exercises as Day 1.

DAY 3: As Day 1, but clock yourself over a mile of walk-trot. Don't race it, but if you beat 12 minutes, you have reached Step 6 in Table 7.

DAY 4: Fast 2-mile walk. Aim at 30 minutes (Step 7). Flexibility and strength exercises as Day 1.

WEEK 7
Exercise three or four times a week. Level C or D.

DAY 1: 45 minutes of steady walking or other Level D activity. 6–8 minutes of flexibility exercises, doing one below the maximum number for each. 3 minutes of strength exercises, doing the minimum number for each.

DAY 2: 15 minutes of easy trotting, walking where necessary. Exercises as Day 1.

DAY 3: 2 miles of fast walking. Aim at 30 minutes (Step 7). You are allowed to trot if you want to, but your improved leg muscles and breathing should be able to cope easily with walking at 4 miles an hour.

DAY 4: 1 mile of walk-trot. Aim at under 12 minutes. Flexibility and strength exercises as Day 1.

ALTERNATIVES: 45 minutes of any Level D activity on Day 1 or 3; 15 minutes of Level C on Day 2 or 4.

WEEK 8
Exercise four days a week. Level C or D.

By this time you should have become used to two days a week of jogging sessions. You can substitute another sport on Level C, but try to jog at least once a week, and remember that the activity, although not flat out, should involve continuous movement (see Chapter 8). You must reach the appropriate steps shown before moving on to Week 9.

DAY 1: 30 minutes of fast walking. Don't worry about exact distance. Flexibility exercises—one complete set, at maximum number for each; plus strength exercises—one set of the

123

basic three, doing one more than the minimum number of each.

DAY 2: 20 minutes of easy walk-trot. Go out for 10 minutes, then turn around and come home in the same time. Set of flexibility and strength exercises, as Day 1, in 9–10 minutes.

DAY 3: One set of flexibility exercises, slowly. Walk for 5 minutes, stretching the muscles, then do 1 mile of walk-trot. Aim at 10 minutes (Step 8 in Table 7). If you feel puffed, walk slowly for 5 minutes afterward.

DAY 4: This is your second endurance challenge. Walk 3 miles briskly. Aim at 45 minutes (Step 9). One set of flexibility and strength exercises as Day 1.

ALTERNATIVES: 40–60 minutes of Level D exercise for Days 1 and 4; 20 minutes of Level C for Day 2. Day 3 is an assessment session and should not be missed. (If you cannot fit in the timed sessions in Week 8 but substitute something else, then you will have to repeat Week 8 before moving on.)

WEEK 9

Four sessions a week. Level C or D. Total amount: 3 hours of D or equivalent.

DAY 1: 1½ miles walk-trot. Aim at 18 minutes (Step 10). One set of flexibility exercises in 6 minutes and one set of strength exercises, doing two more than the minimum of each.

DAY 2: 20 minutes of easy walk-trot. Don't worry about the distance. Exercises as Day 1.

DAY 3: An endurance session. Walk continuously for one hour. Find somewhere nice. One set of flexibility exercises.

DAY 4: Walk-trot 1½ miles. Aim at 16 minutes (Step 11). Exercises as Day 1. This is not meant to be desperately hard —just a method of measuring progress. If you cannot manage it without strain, repeat the week.

WEEK 10

Four sessions a week. Level C or D. Total amount: 3½ hours of D or equivalent.

DAY 1: Another endurance session. Work out a 4-mile walk and try to cover it in 1 hour (Step 12). You should not need to trot at all, but you may if you like. One set of flexibility exercises, slowly.

DAY 2: 30 minutes of walk-trot or another Level C exercise. One set of flexibility exercises in 5–6 minutes, plus one set of strength exercises, in the middle of the range for each.

DAY 3: One set of flexibility exercises, walk 5 minutes, then walk-trot 1½ miles. Aim at 15 minutes (Step 13). Walk around for 5 minutes to get your breath back.

DAY 4: As Day 2, but with a change of surroundings or a change of exercise.

ALTERNATIVES: If you decide to fit in something else, for example an hour of beach football or nine holes of golf instead of Day 1, then make sure you can achieve those steps before moving on to the next week. It is imperative at all times that you be honest with yourself.

WEEK 11

Four sessions a week. Level B, C or D. Total amount: 3½ hours of D or equivalent.

DAY 1: 1 hour of brisk walking or other Level D activity. Flexibility exercises as in Week 10, but increase the number of repetitions of each strength exercise by one and add a fourth strength exercise.

DAY 2: Approximately 2 miles of walk-trot—about 25 minutes. Exercises as Day 1.

DAY 3: Your first day at Level B, which is more strenuous. Try jogging 1 mile continuously, without stopping to walk, then walk 1 mile back, stretching your muscles gently and getting your breath back.

DAY 4: As Day 2, but with a different kind of exercise, for example table tennis; or 1½ miles of trot-walk. Aim at 14 minutes (Step 14). Flexibility and strength exercises as Day 1.

WEEK 12

Four sessions a week. Level B, C or D. Total amount: 4 hours of D or equivalent.

DAY 1: 1½ miles of continuous trotting. Your trotting speed will be about 8–9 minutes per mile, so 12–15 minutes will be ample for a start. Flexibility exercises, one set in 5 minutes, then four strength exercises, at just below the maximum number for each.

DAY 2: 30 minutes of walk-trot. Exercises as Day 1.

DAY 3: Another endurance session. Use the 4-mile walk, which you previously did in 1 hour, and try to do it 5 minutes faster. This will mean breaking into a gentle trot on the downhill bits and keeping up a brisk walk the rest of the way. You have reached Step 15 now.

DAY 4: As Day 2, or another level C activity for half an hour. Exercises as Day 1.

MAINTENANCE SCHEDULE FOR PLAN 1

Your level of activity should be up to four 30-minute sessions of Level C, or their equivalent. You can substitute 20 minutes of continuous trotting for this, or an hour of walking or some other Level D activity. As for the exercises, try to do six sets of flexibility exercises per week, and three or four sets of strength exercises, doing four exercises, using the maximum number shown for each exercise.

As far as targets and challenges are concerned, you should not try to go further than Step 20 on this schedule. If you are capable of exercising four times a week, of jogging 2 miles in 20 minutes or less and of covering 4 miles in 10 minutes under an hour, then you have achieved something that is worthwhile. You are certainly fitter than the average forty-to-fifty-year-old, and you will be able to cope far better with the demands of day-to-day living.

If you are now getting enthusiastic about the active way of life and would like to take part in fairly strenuous weekly sports activities, you ought to move on to Plan 2. If you have repeated Week 12 or the maintenance schedule *twice*, you may move on to Week 5 of Plan 2.

PLAN 2 THE STANDARD PLAN FOR THE WEEKLY ATHLETE

The standard plan is set out for a twelve-week period, with a maintenance schedule at the end to keep up the level of fitness. The plan is arranged in a carefully graduated series of steps, with an increase in the level of training about every two weeks, progress being measured by the "steps to fitness" given in Chapter 7. It is vital that you be able to cope with the demands of one week before moving on to the next. The guide to how much you can take should be that you are completely recovered from each session by the time you are due to do the next session. If you find that one week is rather hard, do not move on, but repeat that week. Racing through the plan is foolish, particularly if you are over forty. It is much better to go at your own speed and reach the top in sixteen or twenty weeks than to break down after ten weeks with a muscle pull and have to start from scratch.

The plan is just a plan, not an order. You start from something that is deliberately quite easy and work your way on to something that would have been very hard at the start of the course. It is the sum of all the weeks' activities that is important, not just one single day. Don't fool yourself that because you can achieve, say, Step 40 in your first week, with a tremendous effort, this represents your true fitness level. The steps should entail no self-punishment; you should be able to take them in your stride.

The plan is arranged in weekly units, and the days in that week may be done in any order. Try to space them out so that you have a day's rest, an important part of the training, after the harder days.

127

WEEK 1
Level C or D. Total amount: 1½ hours of C or equivalent.

DAY 1: 15 minutes trotting, walking for 50 yards or so when you feel out of breath. Do not exceed the stated dose—there is plenty more to come. One set of flexibility exercises, doing the maximum number for each, taking your time. One set of the basic three strength exercises, doing the minimum number.

DAY 2: An hour's walking. Get a good pair of shoes, step out and aim to walk 4 miles in an hour (Step 12). Flexibility and strength exercises as Day 1.

DAY 3: One set of flexibility exercises. Trot-walk 1½ miles. Aim at 15 minutes (Step 13). If you cannot measure 1½ miles, do a mile in 10 minutes, turn around and continue at the same pace for 5 more minutes, then walk the rest.

DAY 4: One set of flexibility and strength exercises as Day 1 in the morning, plus your weekly game in the afternoon.

WEEK 2
Level C or D. Total amount: 3½ hours of D or equivalent.

DAY 1: 20 minutes trotting, walking when necessary. Don't get yourself overtired. Flexibility and strength exercises at the same level and amount as Week 1.

DAY 2: Repeat the distance of last week's walk, but in a different place if possible, and try to go a little faster, trotting the downhill bits if you want to. Aim at 4 miles in 55 minutes (Step 15). This hour on the move is stamina-building. One set of flexibility and strength exercises.

DAY 3: Repeat the trot-walk over 1½ miles. Aim at 14 minutes (Step 14). One set of flexibility and strength exercises as Week 1.

DAY 4: One set of flexibility and strength exercises in the morning. Weekly game in the afternoon. If you are playing football or hockey for 90 minutes you will see from Table 9 (page

115) that this really counts as a Level C exercise and therefore makes up most of the recommended dose for this early stage of the plan. However, you have got to start getting used to training, in small doses at first, and it would be stupid to give up the sport you enjoy just to make the schedule look tidy. Later in the plan the weekly game will be taken at its full value. Similarly, sports like squash should not be dropped just because they are Level B.

If you are under thirty or a regular game player over thirty, the first two weeks will not have overextended you. This is fine. Don't rush it. We are building up gradually to a much higher level of fitness than you have at present.

WEEK 3
Level B, C or D. Total amount: 2 hours of C or equivalent.

DAY 1: One set of flexibility exercises, doing them thoroughly, but getting through in 6–7 minutes. One set of the basic three strength exercises, doing one more than the minimum of each. 25 minutes of trot-walk, not pushing too hard.

DAY 2: One set of flexibility exercises, 6–7 minutes. An hour's walk in 55 minutes—if you see what I mean (4 miles).

DAY 3: Trot-walk 2 miles. Aim at 22 minutes (Step 16). This may be a little more demanding than last week, but don't overexert yourself. If it is a strain, repeat the week. One set each of flexibility and strength exercises as Day 1.

DAY 4: One set each of flexibility and strength exercises in the morning. Weekly game in the afternoon.

WEEK 4
Level B, C or D. Total amount: 2 hours of C or equivalent.

DAY 1: 25 minutes of trotting and walking. Don't worry about the distance covered. One set of flexibility exercises in 6–7 minutes. One set of strength exercises, doing two more than the minimum number of each.

DAY 2: Pick a 4-mile course, preferably in interesting

129

country (but it can be around the park) and try to do it in 50 minutes (Step 18). This will mean walking briskly most of the time and trotting short stretches.

DAY 3: Another measurement session. Trot-walk 2 miles and aim at 20 minutes (Step 17). If it does not come easily, repeat the week. You may find at this stage that the longer, slower stuff comes quite easily, but the 10-minute-mile speed is harder to manage. This is to be expected, since we are trying to improve your heart/lung capacity. Most people have the general endurance to cover a flat 4 miles, and the oxygen demand is not very great at that speed.

DAY 4: One set each of flexibility and strength exercises as Day 1. Weekly game. If no game this week, then 20 minutes of continuous easy trotting, not worrying about distance covered.

WEEK 5
Level B, C or D. Total amount: 2½ hours of C or equivalent.

The schedule is now becoming a little more demanding. You are being asked to do more work, and you can achieve it by increasing either the quality or the quantity. If you feel that it is the speed which you are finding difficult, increase the quantity. If on the other hand you are short of time but can manage the increased pace, then do the same amount faster. If a week is difficult, repeat it—twice if necessary. Your body will gradually adjust itself and become fitter.

DAY 1: 30 minutes of trot-walk. One set of flexibility exercises in 6 minutes; one set of the basic three strength exercises, doing the middle-of-the-range number of each, and add a fourth exercise.

DAY 2: 20 minutes of continuous trotting on your 2-mile course. You should do this comfortably in under 19 minutes (Step 19). One set of flexibility exercises.

DAY 3: 30 minutes of slow but continuous trotting, or 40 minutes of trot-walk, without worrying about the distance. Exercise as Day 1.

DAY 4: Flexibility and strength exercises in the morning. Weekly game in the afternoon. As you get fitter you will be able to put more into this. You will therefore get more out of it, from the fitness angle, but always give yourself a chance to recover before throwing yourself into more training.

WEEK 6
Level B, C or D. Total amount: 3 hours of C or 2 hours of B or equivalent.

You may have started the B level of exercise in Week 4, though there was nothing to stop you from bringing it in in Week 3 if you could manage it. Week 5 had one or two continuous jogging sessions, and provided you can manage it, Week 6 should have two.

DAY 1: 30 minutes of continuous trotting, covering a little more ground than last week. One set of flexibility exercises in 5–6 minutes and one set of four strength exercises.

DAY 2: Trot-walk 1 mile, then rest for 5 minutes. Trot 1½ miles and aim at 13 minutes (Step 20). If you can do this you are certainly getting somewhere. One set of flexibility exercises.

DAY 3: Another endurance session over a 4-mile course. Try to walk-trot this in 45 minutes. As this is slower than 11 minutes per mile, it should be well within your powers by now (Step 21). Exercises as Day 1.

DAY 4: Exercises as Day 1 in the morning, plus your weekly game in the afternoon. As you will be getting fitter, this is now counted as an hour of Level C exercise. This means that it is equivalent to covering 5 miles in an hour.

WEEK 7
Level B, C or D. Total amount: 3 hours of C or 2 hours of B or equivalent.

This week is consolidating the previous one, and moving up slightly in quality.

DAY 1: 35 minutes of continuous trotting. Try to enjoy

131

it. One set of flexibility exercises in 5 minutes, plus a set of four strength exercises, doing two below the maximum number of each.

DAY 2: 1 mile of easy trot-walk as a warm-up. Rest 5 minutes, then trot the 1½-mile course and aim at 12 minutes (Step 22). Exercises as Day 1.

DAY 3: 3 miles of continuous trotting. Aim at 32 minutes (Step 23). This should be easy, compared with the 8-minute-mile speed of the previous session. One set of flexibility and strength exercises as Day 1.

DAY 4: Exercises in the morning, as Day 1, plus weekly game in the afternoon—1 hour-plus of a Level C game or 30 minutes of a Level B game.

WEEK 8
Level A, B or C. Total amount: 2 hours 20 minutes of B or equivalent.

For the first time in the plan we are moving on to the Level A kind of exercise. This is strenuous and should not be attempted until you have achieved all the previous steps. Do not deceive yourself about the speed of your jogging; it is better to build up gradually, by repeating weeks, if you are not confident of your fitness. If you have the time, there is no reason why you should not continue with Level D exercise, but from now on it will not be included in the schedules. The Level A speed, which is anything faster than 8 miles an hour (7½ minutes per mile), is definitely running as opposed to jogging. It will be introduced first as easy Fartlek (see Chapter 8, page 117).

DAY 1: 35 minutes of easy continuous jogging, covering over 3 miles. Increase the amount of flexibility exercise by doing two sets of exercises, with the minimum number of each; these may be done at two separate times of the day, or else before and after the set of four strength exercises. The latter should be done at one below the maximum number for each.

DAY 2: Double set of flexibility exercises; 20 minutes of easy Fartlek. Jog continuously, but put in the occasional 100 yards at a faster pace. Pick up your knees and increase your stride length, and when you feel the pressure, slow back to your gentle jog-trot.

DAY 3: Trot-walk 1 mile to warm up, then trot your 2-mile course continuously. Aim at 18 minutes (Step 24). Flexibility and strength exercises as Day 1.

DAY 4: Exercises in morning. If you have not already done it, get out into the country and try to cover 5 miles in an hour, trotting and walking (Step 25). With the eight weeks of training you now have behind you, this should not be any harder than your hour of weekly sport. If you are feeling tough, go on and cover more miles—anything up to 8 miles, but keep the pace slow: 4 or 5 miles an hour.

WEEK 9
Level A, B or C. Total amount: 2 hours 40 minutes of B or equivalent.

In the last four weeks of this plan, the level of training goes on increasing, and it will not be possible for everyone to keep up with it week by week. The total amount should not be a problem, but achieving the various steps may be. Each time you move up a step it means that your fitness has improved measurably—either in oxygen intake capacity, in heart fitness or in endurance. These changes occur at different rates in different people. You may find it easier to repeat each week, and to move up the steps at half the rate on the plan. It doesn't matter how long it takes you so long as you get there.

DAY 1: 30 minutes of easy Fartlek. Two sets of flexibility exercises, doing one more than the minimum of each. Four strength exercises, doing the maximum number of each.

DAY 2: 1 mile of walk-trot as a warm-up. Jog over the 2-mile course, aiming at under 17 minutes. If you achieve 17 minutes, repeat the week and go for 16 minutes. If you achieve 16 minutes (Step 27), go on to Week 10. Exercises as Day 1.

DAY 3: Flexibility exercises. 3 miles continuous jog, aiming at 30 minutes (Step 28).

DAY 4: Flexibility and strength exercises in morning. Weekly game, 80–90 minutes of Level C or 40–45 minutes of Level B.

WEEK 10
Level A, B or C. Total amount: 2 hours 40 minutes of B or equivalent.

No increase in the volume of training, but an increase in quality. Repeat the week until you can manage all the steps.

DAY 1: An endurance session: 4 miles, trotting gently most of the way. Aim at 42 minutes (Step 29). Two sets of flexibility exercises as in Week 9, in about 10 minutes. One set of five strength exercises, doing the minimum number of each.

DAY 2: Fartlek: 2½ miles continuous jogging with bursts of striding out. Aim at 20 minutes (Step 30). If it is difficult to measure 2½ miles accurately, aim at 3 miles in 27 minutes (Step 31). Flexibility exercises only.

DAY 3: Exercises as Day 1. 20 minutes of easy Fartlek or 40 minutes of a Level B exercise.

DAY 4: Exercises as Day 1. 40 minutes slow, continuous jogging in different country, or weekly game.

WEEK 11
Level A, B or C. Total amount: 3 hours of B or equivalent.

There is another rise in total amount of work here, which you can best meet by increasing the number of Level A sessions. In this way you get the most training effect with the least amount of time spent. However, if you feel you are not fit enough, repeat Week 10 before moving on.

DAY 1: 20 minutes of Fartlek. This is not very long, so you should be able to fit in several bursts of 100 yards at a striding speed. Two sets of flexibility exercises in 10 minutes, plus one set of five strength exercises, doing two more than the minimum number.

DAY 2: 10 minutes walk-trot to warm up. One set of flexibility exercises, done slowly. 3 miles continuous run, aiming at 25 minutes (Step 32).

DAY 3: Exercises as Day 1. 4 miles steady trot. Aim at breaking 40 minutes (Step 33). As this is only a 10-minute-mile pace, much slower than the Fartlek runs, you ought by now to be able to manage it.

DAY 4: Exercises as Day 1 in morning. Weekly game, or 40–45 minutes of jogging, without worrying about the distance.

WEEK 12
Level A, B or C. Total amount: 1 hour 40 minutes of A or equivalent.

By the time you come to the end of Week 12, you should have reached a stage where you can run three times a week without torturing yourself. The running speed of Level A is anything faster than 7½ minutes a mile.

DAY 1: 25 minutes of Fartlek, running stretches of 200 yards at a good pace and dropping to a slow jog when you feel the strain. Two sets of flexibility exercises in 10 minutes, plus a set of five strength exercises, doing the average number for each.

DAY 2: Flexibility exercises. 3 miles continuous run. Aim at 24 minutes (Step 34).

DAY 3: Flexibility and strength exercises in the morning, as Day 1. Fartlek session as Day 1, or 45–50 miutes of a Level B sport.

DAY 4: Exercises as Day 1. Weekly game or else attempt Step 35. This is an endurance session, 5 miles in 50 minutes. Find some interesting country to jog in, and look on it as a challenge.

MAINTENANCE SCHEDULE FOR PLAN 2
To fit in with your way of life, the flexibility and strength exercises may be split up, so that on three or four mornings a week you do

two sets of flexibility exercises (10 minutes) and on three mornings a week you do the set of five strength exercises mentioned above, working up to the maximum number of each. The running program should include two 25-minute Fartlek sessions, and one straight run of 2 or 3 miles against the clock. If the weekly game is missed, then a longish but slow 4–5-mile trot may be put in. This pattern can be continued indefinitely. Your target for this level should be to reach Step 40 on the scale—4 miles at just over 8 minutes a mile—and 2 miles in 15 minutes. From the point of view of stamina, you should be able to cover 8 miles in under 2 hours. If you are filled with ambition to go further, you can go on to Week 3 of Plan 3 after two weeks of the maintenance schedule.

PLAN 3   THE ADVANCED FITNESS PLAN

This plan is both for those who have worked their way up from Plan 2 and for those who are already quite fit. An under-thirty game player, who is engaging in his sport or training for it twice a week, should be perfectly capable of running 3 miles at a steady trot in under 25 minutes (Step 32 in Table 7). As far as his stamina goes, he should be able to cover 5 miles in an hour without feeling any aftereffects. What this schedule is designed to do is bring him to a point where his maximum oxygen intake (see Chapter 8) will allow him to run at 6 minutes per mile and at the same time increase his endurance, muscular strength and flexibility.

This schedule will not be for everyone, because it is aimed at general fitness, particularly heart fitness. It will, however, bring to whoever follows it a degree of all-around fitness far above anything the ordinary man attains. The emphasis throughout the book is on *general* fitness with a view to survival, so specialist athletes who want to train for their event will need to add such elements as circuit training, weight training, skill training and event practice.

Age is no barrier here, provided the training is taken step by step, and there are hundreds of the physically active, many of them over forty, who would consider these schedules a mere "doddle." There are some marathon runners of over fifty who can run the twenty-six miles at faster than six minutes per mile.

The plan, arranged in a carefully graduated series of steps, with an increase in the level of training, is set out for a twelve-week period, with a maintenance schedule at the end. The progress is measured by reference to the "One Hundred Steps to Superfitness" given in Chapter 7. It is vital that you be able to cope with the demands of one week before moving on to the next. If necessary, repeat a week two or three times before going on to the next level.

Remember that the plan is not a command. You are doing this for your own benefit, to improve your health and to help you to get more out of life. The exercise should include a lot of the things you enjoy doing.

When you are following the plan for a particular week you may take the individual days in any order, but it is advisable to follow a hard session with either a rest day or an easy day. The body must have this rest in order to benefit from the training; all top athletes know this. However, there is no reason why the flexibility and strength exercises should not be done at a different time of day from the other training, so long as they are done. Later in the schedule you will find that you are encouraged to do these exercises five or six days a week; the running or other exercises, four or five times.

When you are attempting the various steps, do not regard them as races. They should not be flat-out efforts, but just part of the weekly training, literally taken in your stride. The steps mentioned in the schedules need not be rigidly adhered to. Some of those doing the plan will have much more running ability than others and will move much more quickly up the steps. On the other hand, the *volume* of training *should* be adhered to.

If you suffer a muscle strain or other injury, refer to Chapter 10 and take the appropriate action.

137

WEEK 1

Four sessions a week. Level B, C or D. Total amount: 3 hours of Level C or D, or 2 hours of Level B (or a mixture).

In the first two weeks of this course we are trying to build up the stamina to take the training load that will come later on. Even though you may be quite fit, from your assessment of yourself, for one single session, your legs may not be tough enough to take continuous training. We therefore start with longer, slower sessions.

DAY 1: 30 minutes steady jogging, stopping to walk only if you really feel bad. Distance should be over 3 miles. Flexibility exercises—one set, taking them slowly, doing the maximum number for each.

DAY 2: 1 hour of easy walking and jogging or a Level C game such as tennis. One set of flexibility exercises as Day 1, plus one set of five strength exercises, doing the minimum number for each.

DAY 3: 20 minutes jogging at a brisk pace (10 minutes out and back). Exercises as Day 2.

DAY 4: 1–2 hours of either brisk walking, walking and jogging, or some level C sport. Exercises as Day 2.

WEEK 2

Four sessions a week. Level B, C or D. Total amount: 4 hours of Level C or D, or three hours of Level B.

This continues the Week 1 process and gets you used to spending 3–4 hours on your feet taking exercise every week.

DAY 1: 40 minutes of easy jogging, covering over 4 miles. Two sets of flexibility exercises, doing the minimum number of each.

DAY 2: Go out 2 miles, at an easy jog or walk-trot, and then run 2 miles back. Compare the time with the table. It should be under 15 minutes (Step 37). Flexibility exercises as Day 1, plus one set of five strength exercises, doing the average number of each.

DAY 3: As Day 1, or 40 minutes of some Level B exercise such as squash.

DAY 4: 1–2 hours of walking, walking and jogging, or some Level C game such as football. Exercises as Day 2.

WEEK 3

Level A, B or C. Four sessions a week. Total amount: 3 hours of B or 1½ hours of A, or equivalent.

From now on, Level D exercise does not count as part of the training. Most of it will be Level A or B, but if you engage in a Level C sport this can be counted into the week's total.

DAY 1: 30-minute run. Start off gently and build up to a steady jog—15 minutes out and 15 minutes back. Ease down to a slow jog in the last 3 minutes. Flexibility exercises—two sets, doing the average number of each. Strength exercises—one set of five, doing the same number as last week.

DAY 2: Work out a 3-mile course. Do your flexibility exercises as Day 1. Walk-trot for 5 minutes to loosen up, then run your 3 miles and time yourself. Aim for under 22 minutes (Step 38).

DAY 3: 45 minutes of a Level B sport or form of training. Exercises as Day 1.

DAY 4: Another stamina-building session. Try to get in a good hour's walk-trotting at the weekend, doing 5 miles. Find some nice countryside. Exercises as Day 1.

WEEK 4

Level A, B or C. Four sessions a week. Total amount: 3½ hours of B or 2 hours of A or equivalent.

The emphasis is now changing toward shorter, faster sessions.

DAY 1: A 4-mile run. This training distance is going to be used a lot, so try to measure it accurately, preferably on a circular course. Do your flexibility exercises first—two sets, doing the maximum number for each. Take the first mile gently, then get up to the best speed you can comfortably manage. Ease down in the last half-mile or so. Time yourself. Under 35 minutes is Step 39.

DAY 2: 45–60 minutes of a Level B activity, or 1½ hours of a Level C sport. Exercises as Day 1, plus strength exercises—one set of five, doing the average number for each.

DAY 3: A short, fast run. Do your exercises as Day 2, then about 10 minutes of walking and trotting to loosen up. Run 2 miles and aim at 14 minutes (Step 41).

DAY 4: A steady 4 miles, or 35 minutes, running only as fast as you feel like running. Exercises as Day 2.

WEEK 5

Level A, B or C. Four sessions a week. Total amount: 3½ hours of B or 2 hours of A or equivalent.

From now on there is little change in the recommended amount of strength and flexibility training, until the suggestions in Week 9. The daily routine should consist of two sets of flexibility exercises, doing the maximum number for each. These can be done with the main training or separately. They should be completed in 10 minutes, if done thoroughly. The strength exercises, five of them, should be built up to the maximum number shown for each, and one set of five should suffice. Try to do both these sets of exercises five days a week or, at the very least, three days a week.

DAY 1: Have another go at your 4-mile circuit, trying to knock a bit off your time. Under 33 minutes is Step 40; under 31 minutes is Step 42.

DAY 2: Try another activity—50–60 minutes of Level B, or 1½ hours of a Level C sport.

DAY 3: A brisk 20-minute run, but spend the first 5 minutes going slowly, then try to speed up a bit when you get warm. Jog the last 2 minutes slowly.

DAY 4: Aim to increase your stamina by covering approximately 5 miles. Don't worry about time, but keep going.

WEEK 6

Four or five sessions a week. Level A, B or C. Total amount: 3½–4 hours of B or 2–2½ hours of A.

During the past three weeks you have been getting used to regular nonstop runs, and have also found out your performances over various courses from 2 to 5 miles. The Week 6 program represents a balanced program of straight runs (which may be repeated week after week) that will gradually make you fitter and bring down the times for your courses. It will not take up very much of your week, nor should it upset your normal pattern of life. By the end of Week 5 you should be feeling much fitter, and your legs should be strong enough to take the equivalent of five 30-minute sessions a week. One word of warning: Don't get so set into the routine that it becomes boring. No two days in a week should be alike.

DAY 1: Run for about 30 minutes, on a basis of 15 minutes out and 15 minutes back, or go around a 4-mile course.

DAY 2: An alternative sport or exercise, for example squash, for 45–60 minutes. As you become fitter you will be playing at a higher work rate and, strictly speaking, need not do quite so much from the training point of view. A really hard game would count as a Level A activity.

DAY 3: A short, fast run, after warming up for 10 minutes (see Chapter 10), in the region of 20–21 minutes for 3 miles (Steps 44 and 50).

DAY 4: A slow, stamina-building run, 5 miles in 40–45 minutes (Steps 43 and 47).

Time yourself and record your progress on one day a week.

DAY 5: Either 1½ hours of a Level C sport such as hockey or football, or some kind of outdoor challenge—for example, an hour's orienteering, a hill climb, or a 5- or 6-mile cross-country trek.

141

NATURAL FITNESS

WEEK 7
Level A, B or C. Four or five sessions a week. Total amount: 2–2½ hours of A or equivalent.

If you have been repeating the Week 6 program, your times will improve quite fast at first over your courses, but then you will reach a plateau. You can then make further progress either by increasing the time spent on training, which may be inconvenient and boring, or by improving the quality of the sessions. Here we start moving into the realms of the serious athlete.

DAY 1: A straight run around a 5-mile course, or about 35 minutes' continuous exercise.

DAY 2: An easy Fartlek session. Run at a steady jog on a 3-mile course. After the first 5 minutes put in bursts of faster running, lasting 30 seconds or 150 yards, and then drop back to your jog. Put in a 30-second burst every 2 minutes.

DAY 3: A short, fast run around a 2- or 3-mile course.

DAY 4: An easy interval session. Find a playing field or open area, say 600 yards round the perimeter, and pace out 200 yards. Jog three times round the field to loosen up, do your exercises, then do six laps, putting in a fast burst over 200 yards, followed by a slow jog for the remaining 400 yards.

DAY 5: 45 minutes of a Level B activity, or as Day 5 in Week 6.

Time yourself and record progress on one day.

WEEK 8
Level A, B or C. Four or five sessions a week. Total amount: 2½ hours of Level A or equivalent.

This week brings in a little more of the track runner's kind of training.

DAY 1: A Fartlek session lasting 30 minutes. After the warm-up period, put in bursts of faster running lasting a minute or

142

300 yards, then jog until recovered after each one. When tired cut the bursts down to 30 seconds.

DAY 2: A straight timed run over a 3- or 4-mile course.

DAY 3: A hill session. This is a very good method of getting fit, but it is hard work and is not to be done unless you are in really good condition. Pick a hill about 100–200 yards long and 50–100 feet high. This will be steep enough to make you work, but not so steep as to bring you to a standstill. Run up it steadily, keeping going, however slowly, to the top; then walk down to the bottom. Do this eight times. Later you can build this up to ten, twelve or even fifteen times.

DAY 4: A 6-mile, stamina-building trot. Time it occasionally.

DAY 5: Something different. Either one of your other sports or some kind of outdoor challenge. By now you should be fit enough to jog 10 miles or to walk 20 miles cross-country. Find some good country and have a go.

WEEK 9

Level A, B or C. Four or five sessions a week. Total amount: 2½–3 hours of A per week.

The problems you are having to overcome are those of raising your tempo to higher speeds and adjusting yourself to absorbing more training. Weeks 7 and 8 brought in three different kinds of running: Fartlek, interval training and hill running. These can be expanded in Weeks 9 and 10, but remember not to move on a week until you feel that you have mastered the previous week's work. By measuring yourself over courses of 4, 5 or 6 miles you will be able to see improvement in both stamina and oxygen intake.

One new suggestion here is the use of circuit training. This can be put in instead of the strength exercises at any time and, once you are used to it, can count as part of your weekly program as Level A (when you are starting it, however, count it as Level B). It is particularly useful in the winter, when you don't feel like

143

training outside in the dark. See Chapter 11 for more details.

DAY 1: 30-minute run, not timed.

DAY 2: Hill session, increasing to doing twelve times up your hill, jogging slowly down to recover each time.

DAY 3: Easy Fartlek, doing a few fast strides with long recovery jogs in between.

DAY 4: Warm-up exercises and then a time trial over a 3- or 4-mile course.

DAY 5: 1½ hours of another sport, or else an outdoor challenge—mountain walk, orienteering.

WEEK 10

This is an alternative program that can follow straight on from Week 9 at the same work load.

DAY 1: Interval training; 1 mile of jogging; exercises; then eight times 300 yards at a good pace, with a 300-yard jog after each.

DAY 2: 20-minute untimed run.

DAY 3: 40-minute Fartlek run, on road or cross-country. Start off doing 1 minute fast, 2 minutes slow, then after 20 minutes cut down to 30 seconds fast, 1 minute slow.

DAY 4: Warm-up exercises, then time trial around a 5- or 6-mile course.

DAY 5: Long and easy cross-country trek, or some kind of prolonged outdoor sport.

If you have followed the sessions this far, you will have reached a high state of fitness. Whether you are running fast times for your courses will depend on whether you have the build to be a long-distance runner; but what is certain is that your leg strength, your endurance and, in particular, your "heart fitness," or maximum oxygen intake, will be far above what they were when you started.

WEEK 11

Four or five sessions a week. Level A or B. Total amount: 3 hours.

DAY 1: Interval training on grass. Warm-up exercises, then ten times 300 yards fast (speed about 5 minutes per mile) followed by 300-yard jog each time.

DAY 2: 30-minute cross-country run, covering over 4 miles.

DAY 3: 6 miles Fartlek in 42–45 minutes, doing 1 minute fast, 1 minute slow, then 30 seconds fast, 30 seconds slow; last half-mile at steady jog.

DAY 4: Time trial over 5 or 6 miles, or take part in some sort of race.

DAY 5: Long easy run, about 8 miles in an hour.

WEEK 12

Four or five sessions a week. Level A or B. Total amount: 3 hours.

DAY 1: Hill running or resistance running (see Chapter 8, page 116)—e.g., six times 600 yards through sand dunes.

DAY 2: Easy Fartlek over 5 miles, doing short, fast bursts (faster than 5-minute-mile speed) over 100 yards, with long recovery sessions in between.

DAY 3: Repetition running (see Chapter 8, page 116). Warm-up exercises; then, say, four times 880 yards at a fast pace, with 5 minutes' slow jogging after each.

DAY 4: 8-mile run against the clock; check your progress on the chart.

DAY 5: A 30-minute recovery session, jogging easily around the grass, or some different kind of sport.

I would expect anyone who has followed these schedules to be able to keep up a 6-minute-mile speed for 3 miles, and a 7-minute-mile speed for anything up to 8 miles. The question is, How long will it take? If you have followed Plan 2, or started from the same standard of fitness (roughly, Steps 36–40), then after ten weeks I would expect you to be capable of reaching Steps 56–58. This applies to anyone of this fitness standard under the age of forty.

Everyone has his limits, but these limits apply mostly to your maximum speed, not your maximum distance. Almost everyone can work up to a speed of 7 minutes per mile; most to a speed of 6 minutes. After that, it is possible to greatly increase the distance you can cover at your maximum distance-running speed.

These last two weeks are typical of the kind of training done by club athletes all over the world. They occupy thirty minutes a day on four days of the week, plus one hour at the weekend. In addition I would expect that the exercises for strength and flexibility would be kept up and done four or five times a week, occupying an extra ten to fifteen minutes a day.

If you have done all this, you have come a long way. The hours you spend on training will add years to your span of active life. Don't give up now!

10

Advice on Running Training

CLOTHING

The clothing you wear for exercise must make you as comfortable as possible; you should feel good when you are dressed for training. Furthermore, if you have the right clothing then you can do your training in any weather conditions. For a man, the basic gear is lightweight shorts and undershirt or T-shirt. They should not fit tightly anywhere—this would lead to overheating and chafing. A jockstrap or briefs should be worn under your shorts. This is the minimum that decency generally allows, though if you are training on the beach, just trunks will suffice.

In winter you will need a lot more. A track suit is the best thing, as it allows freedom of movement for your legs and has a close enough weave to make it fairly windproof. On the other hand, you can manage pretty well with just an old pair of trousers and a sweater. Everyone will need a waterproof anorak or parka with hood so that he can go out in the rain on occasions when it is unavoidable. Your track suit or other outer garments, however, are only to keep you warm when you first go out. After you have got through your warm-up period you will be able to take them off. This will help you to run faster. If you are training regularly, you will need two or three sets of running kit and a second set of protective clothing, so that the other stuff can be washed.

FOOTWEAR

This is the only aspect that will cost you anything, so it is worth taking seriously. If your footwear is unsatisfactory, then you may mess up your entire program.

For running on the beach or on soft grass, nature has equipped you with two perfectly adequate feet. These feet have several points over other forms of footwear: they cost nothing, are the lightest, are the easiest to keep clean and are also self-repairing.

However, if you are doing any running over roads, hard ground or cinder tracks, you will need a pair of training shoes. But make sure the shoes are adequate; otherwise you are likely to suffer from bruised heels, blisters and strained arches. A good pair should have a microcellular rubber sole, not very pliable, and there should be foam padding in the heel and also under the arch. The shape of the shoes should approximate the shape of your foot, so that your toes are not swimming in a void anywhere. The uppers should be of soft leather so that they do not chafe your foot when wet.

Ordinary tennis shoes may be all right if extra foam-rubber insoles and heel pads are added, but they will not give enough support to your foot to be any good for long road runs. So-called "road shoes" are probably not a good thing for training, as they are designed for road races and tend to be rather light and flimsy. The same applies to many cross-country shoes. If you are going to do much cross-country training in winter, then get a heavy pair of cross-country studs or a light pair of rubber-studded soccer shoes. The "ripple" type of sole is a good compromise for those who are training in small amounts over varied terrain. A good pair of training shoes is fairly expensive, but they are a very worthwhile investment—an investment in health. There are several good makes; I have personally always used Adidas shoes, and have great faith in them.

The chief purpose of socks is to prevent friction between foot and shoe; they should not, therefore, be too thin. The shoe should fit firmly even without lacing. A sock of a wool-nylon mixture seems to work best; I am still using for training the socks in which I ran across the United States six years ago! If you find blisters a problem, make sure that your shoes are not chafing anywhere. A further useful precaution, used by marathon runners, is to wear a thin stretch-nylon sock inside the ordinary woolen sock. If the foot does slide about at all, the friction is then between sock and sock rather than sock and foot. For treatment of blisters see page 152.

WARMING UP

No experienced athlete would think of starting a training session without warming up first. If you start running fast the moment you get outside the door you are far more likely to get muscle strains. Always start very slowly, at a gentle jogging pace, and do not start running fast until you have jogged half a mile. In cold weather wear track suit or trousers for the first mile or two, until you get really warm. Stiff muscles tear easily and should be treated even more gently. Gentle massage or use of a liniment or rub will help to warm up the muscles, but normally the heat of running is quite enough.

You may see athletes warming up for half an hour before a race, but this is as much psychological preparation as physical. For a training run, five minutes' jogging and five minutes of flexibility exercises will be enough.

RUNNING ACTION

Running is natural. The running action that feels easiest for you is probably the best for you. Do not try to run with long strides like a miler on the track. Do not try to run on your toes. Most long-distance runners land on the ball of the foot, with the heel touching the ground just afterward; as the body weight moves forward the heel comes off the ground, and the push-off comes from the ball of the foot and the toes. The only conscious thought I would suggest on running action is to keep your toes and knees pointed forward as your legs come through, not to swing them out to the side.

The upper part of your body should be carried in the posture that entails the least strain. Your arms will be carried at about hip level, not tensed across the chest. Hands should be closed, not clenched. Your neck and head will be in the same line as your spine, either vertical or with a slight forward lean. Your neck and shoulder muscles should be as relaxed as possible. If you start to feel strain in any part of your body, drop to a gentle jog; let your arms, neck and shoulders relax completely; and then move back to your faster running action.

When you have been running regularly for a few weeks, you will not need to think about posture at all, because you will have found the action and the stride length that suit you best. Everybody is different, so don't be worried if your stride is not the same as somebody else's. When you get fitter and move up to a faster pace, you will find that you will be running with more knee lift and a longer stride, but when you are jogging you should be moving with the minimum of effort.

WHERE TO RUN

You don't need a running track. You can run anywhere if you are determined to, but the pleasanter the place you choose, the more likely you are to keep it up. The roads are the most easily available running places, and this is where long-distance runners do most of their training. Paved roads have the advantages of being unaffected by weather conditions and being lit at night if you live in a town. It is usually possible to find within easy reach of your home one or two small circuits, about one, two or three miles in length, where there is not too much traffic. If there is no footpath, then run facing the traffic, on the left-hand side, so that you can see the vehicle that is approaching.

One of the disadvantages of running on populated roads is the comments of the passers-by. As the encounters tend to be brief, the level of the repartee is never very high—remarks such as "Run, you'll get there!" and "You're too late, it's gone!" A dignified silence is the best defense, particularly if you have little breath to spare.

The other big disadvantage is the hard surface. If you do too much road running you may start to get "shin splints" down the front of your legs. If you are jogging only three times a week and have good training shoes, you will probably be all right, but if you are doing more, then avoid running on roads on two consecutive days. In most parts of the United States it is possible to find a park, recreation ground or golf course. Running on the grass is pleasanter than on a road and far easier on the legs. You can easily work out a course, perhaps of two or three laps, that can be used for assessing your fitness and progress. Beware of dogs and golf balls! Cross-country running, through forest paths and around the edges of fields, is a pleasant diversion, and the changes of footing and scenery make it far less boring than the road.

If you want to run in company, try to find out your nearest athletic club or orienteering club. The latter sport is more encouraging for the beginner, because the standard of fitness is not as high, and you are able to compete at your own level and age group.

Remember that you can run anywhere. Don't make excuses for yourself; make opportunities.

INJURIES

Most of these are caused simply by trying to do too much too quickly, and just as simply cured by doing less, more slowly.

SPLINTS

Pains down the front of the legs, either side of the shinbone. Caused by too much running on hard surfaces, particularly by fast downhill running. Avoid roads for a week and run on grass or sand. Wear training shoes with thicker soles.

BLISTERS

Caused by badly fitting shoes and socks, or by too much friction, particularly in hot weather. (For prevention, see under Footwear.) Whether to puncture or not should be a medical decision, but when medical assistance is not available it is sometimes advisable to puncture a blister before it breaks from friction. (A diabetic should always seek medical advice regarding injuries to the feet.) To puncture a blister, first wash it with soap, then swab with alcohol. Sterilize a needle in a flame and make one opening near the edge of the blister. Press fluid out with gentle pressure. Protect with sterile gauze, then cover with a protective tape such as moleskin. Pack your shoes with extra socks to restrict the movement. "Toughening" your feet with salt water or rubbing alcohol is a waste of time, since old skin is constantly worn away and fresh skin produced.

STIFFNESS

The commonest beginner's ailment. Caused by overuse of the muscles concerned. Prevented by "warming down" after any strenuous effort and by having a warm bath and a change immediately after training. Cured only by taking it easy. Complete rest does less good in assisting recovery than walking or gentle jogging.

MUSCLE PULLS

Caused by overloading the muscle. Prevented by warming up properly (remember: cold and stiff muscles pull easily) and by training in a graduated fashion. Cure: chiefly rest, aided by stimulating the blood flow—use of gentle massage, liniment, hot baths and infrared radiation. Light strapping that takes the strain off the injured muscle may also help. You may exercise it gently, but stop as soon as you feel any pain.

JOINTS

Ligament strains, caused by a sudden twist, or by running on rough ground, respond only to rest and warmth. Swollen knees should be treated carefully. If you sustain a knee injury, it may be aggravated by formation of scar tissue in the knee joint. If this is not dispersed, you may experience recurring knee trouble whenever the knee is in action for a long time. If pain and swelling persist after a week's rest, see a doctor.

ACHILLES TENDON STRAIN

Caused by running faster than you are used to, particularly on hard surfaces, or by "on the toes" exercises such as skipping. Prevented by graduated training and by wearing cushioned training shoes. Cure: wear shoes with good heels, or use cushion heel pads. Jog slowly, or walk, until pain disappears. This is *not* the kind of injury that can be "run off."

STITCH

This is still a mystery, but I think that the most likely cause is pressure in the intestine. Prevented by not overeating before exercise; by allowing over an hour between a meal and an easy jog, and two hours before a serious run. Proper warming up helps to avoid it, and so does adequate training—it occurs more often in the unfit. Cure: stop running and walk, bending your trunk forward and massaging your lower abdomen gently. Breathe deeply and steadily from the stomach.

11

Indoor Training and Exercises

FLEXIBILITY EXERCISES

This set of nine exercises should be done in sequence, without making any movement too fast. The stretching should reach the point of discomfort, but not pain. The varied amounts shown in some of the exercises are on a five-point basis, from minimum to maximum, as referred to in Chapter 9.

F1 NECK ROLLING

Stand with feet about two feet apart, knees straight, stomach held in, hands on hips. Roll head right around, with maximum back and forward neck movement. Five times one way, then five times the other way. (About thirty seconds.)

155

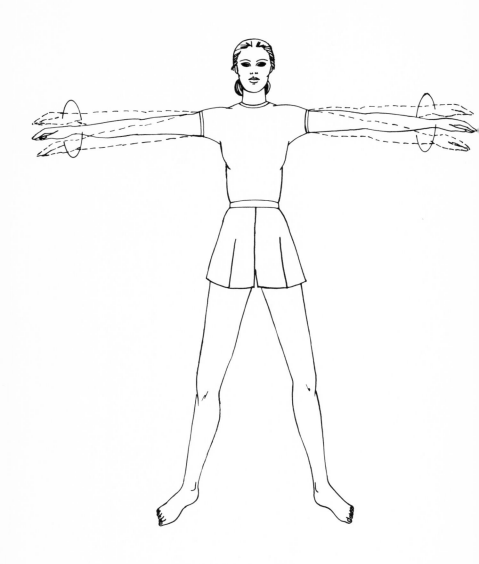

F2 SHOULDER ROTATION
Stand as in F1, with arms out sideways, palms downward. Pulling
the arms back slightly, rotate the hands in small circles, ten times

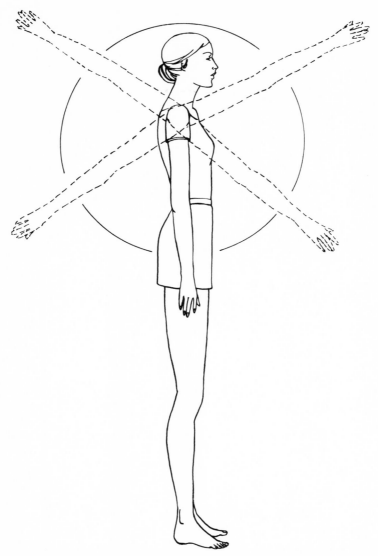

one way and then ten times the other way. Turn the palms upward and repeat. Then, with the arms hanging down, swing both
arms in full circles, with maximum rotation, twelve times one way
and then twelve times the other way.

157

F3 TRUNK ROTATION

Stand as in F1, with your hands on your hips, and breathe deeply, using stomach and chest. Then sway your trunk backward and to the right, leaning back as far as possible but keeping your feet firmly planted on the floor and your knees braced. Swing your trunk around to the left, bend forward and come back to the start. Repeat slowly, six to ten times in each direction.

158

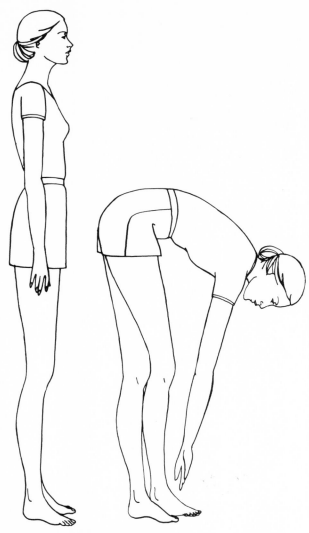

F4 LEG STRETCHING

Stand with feet together, then cross the right foot over the left. Keeping your knees straight, bend over and push your fingers down toward your right toes. Push down ten times, then straighten up, cross the left foot over the right and repeat. Do ten to twenty each side.

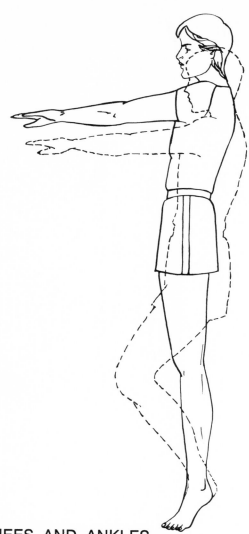

F5 KNEES AND ANKLES

Stand up straight, feet together. Raise your heels off the ground and hold your arms out in front of you, palms downward. Staying on your toes, and keeping your knees close together and your arms outstretched, sink slowly to a knees-bent position, then straighten up slowly. Try to keep your head up and remain balanced. Do this, slowly, six to ten times.

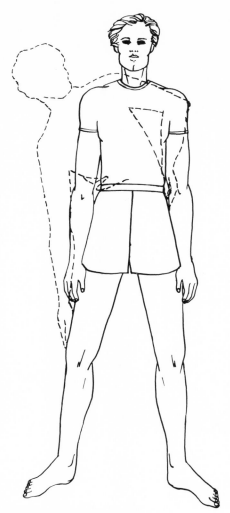

F6 SIDE BENDING (TRUNK)

Stand with feet apart, arms by your sides. Reach down your right side with your extended right hand, keeping your left shoulder pressed back. Push slowly down, then relax. Repeat six to ten times each side.

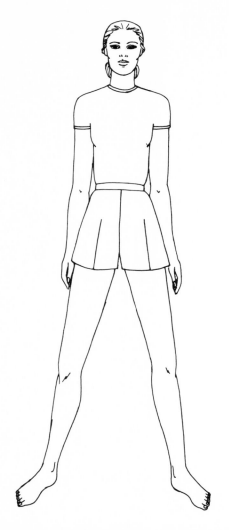

F7 "WINDMILLS" (TRUNK AND SHOULDERS)
Stand with your feet apart, arms hanging by your sides. Turn your body to the left, keeping your feet on the ground and your knees

braced, and at the same time swing both arms up over your left shoulder, keeping them straight and roughly parallel to each other. Swing around to the right. Do this fifteen to twenty times.

163

F8 "LUNGING" (HIPS AND THIGHS)

Adopt the posture of a fencer about to make a lunge to the right. You are facing to the right, with your right knee bent and your left foot out behind you. Lunge forward, bending your right knee and pushing your left leg farther back. Keep on pushing the left leg back, keeping it straight, so that your bottom moves nearer to the ground. Relax, turn to the left and lunge again. Do this six to ten times each side.

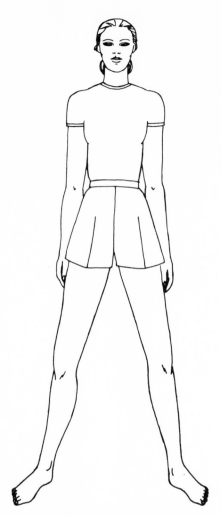

F9 LEG AND SPINE STRETCHING

Stand with feet about two feet apart. Keeping your knees straight, lean forward with your arms hanging down. Lean as far as is comfortable, then press down so that your fingertips touch the ground in front of you. Hold it for two seconds, then relax. Lean and press again. Do this three to eight times. Move your feet to

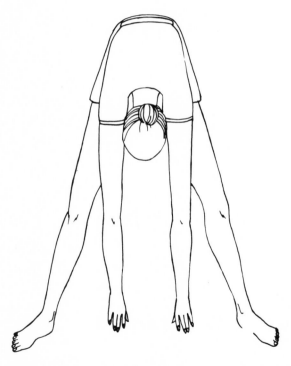

about a yard apart, then repeat the exercise, this time trying to get the palms of your hands on the floor. Do this three to eight times. Finally, move your feet as far apart as they will go and, with folded

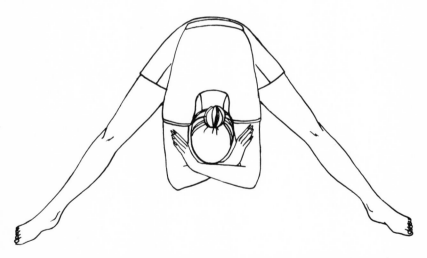

arms, try to press your elbows down to the ground. I find this quite impossible, but more flexible people with shorter legs can do it quite easily.

167

There are literally hundreds of possible flexibility exercises, and if you have some favorite ones you can include them in your regular program. The important thing is that all the main muscle groups should be stretched, and that the routine should be easy to remember. These nine exercises, plus the first three strength exercises, form a good "daily dozen." The next two strength exercises come into the training plans set out in Chapter 9 and can be added when you get fitter.

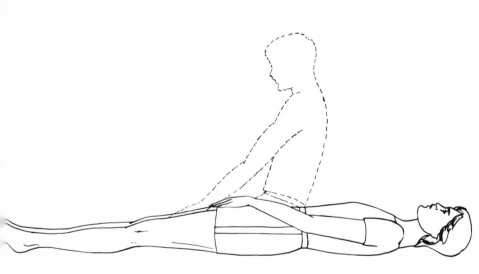

STRENGTH EXERCISES

S1   SIT-UPS

Lie on your back and fold your hands behind your neck. Keeping your legs on the ground, raise your trunk to a sitting position. Repeat eight to twelve times.

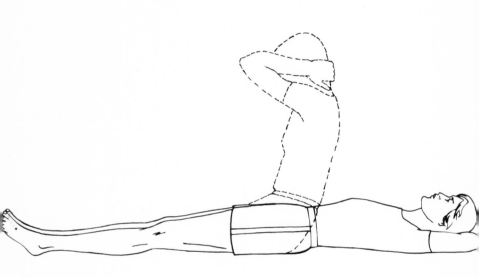

S1A

If you find S1 impossible, lie with your hands on your thighs and, as you raise your trunk, slide your fingers down toward your knees. Repeat eight to twelve times. This one will strengthen your stomach and back muscles in the same way, and eventually you will be able to do the full exercise.

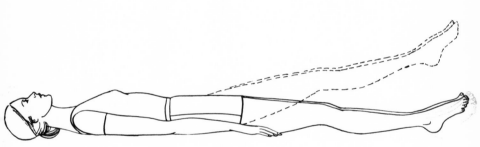

S2 LEG RAISING

Lie on your back with your feet together. Raise your legs, keeping them straight, until your heels are about eighteen inches off the ground. Hold it for three seconds and then lower them slowly. Repeat four to eight times.

171

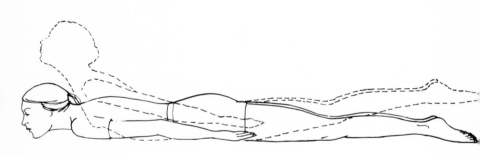

S3 BACK ARCHING

Lie on your stomach with your hands by your sides, palms upward. Tense your back muscles, raise your head and chest off the ground and at the same time try to get your knees and thighs off the ground. You may not move them very far, but the effort will strengthen your back muscles. Repeat four to eight times.

172

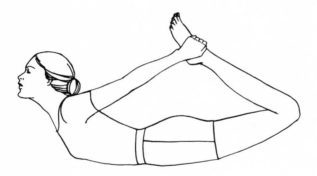

S3A

S3a If you find S3 difficult, bend your knees and grasp your ankles with your hands (still lying on your front). Pull hard on your ankles while lifting your chest off the floor.

173

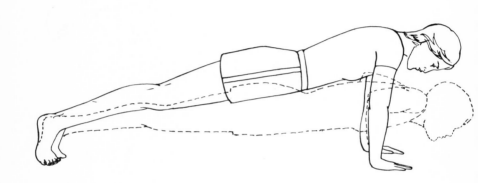

S4 PUSH-UPS

Lying on your front, raise yourself off the ground with your arms and straighten your body and legs so that only your toes and hands are in contact with the ground. Keeping your body straight, bend your arms until your chest is almost on the ground. Repeat ten to twenty times.

N.B.: Not recommended for those with heart complaints or high blood pressure.

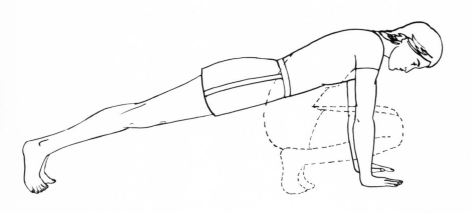

S5 BURPEES

In the push-up position, jump forward so that your knees come up under your chest, then jump back again, shooting your toes backward. Repeat ten to twenty times.

175

CIRCUIT TRAINING AT HOME

Circuit training, an organized course of exercises, provides excellent all-around indoor training. It makes use of a series of exercise stations placed around a room. After doing a prescribed number of repetitions of an exercise at one station, you move, without pause, to the next station. Being quite strenuous, it is more fun done in a group at a Y or health club. However, if you want to try this kind of training at home, the following circuit can be set up with the minimum of apparatus. You need a firm chair or bench, with the seat eighteen to twenty-two inches off the floor; a thick book; two or three bricks; something to hang from, such as the top of the stairs, and a skipping rope (optional).

The session consists of one set of flexibility exercises, three times around the circuit and a heart-training exercise at the end. At the beginning you go twice around the circuit slowly, doing the minimum number of each exercise. When you can get through the circuit three times quickly, increase the number of each exercise. Twice a week of circuit training will be enough, but this can form the major part of your exercise program in the winter, if you add in one run and one game per week. If done flat out, it is a Level A form of exercise, but generally it can be rated as Level B.

I suggest ten exercises, done in a continuous sequence. One set of the first nine exercises is once around the circuit. The tenth, the heart-training exercise, is done after you have done your three complete circuits. The order in which you do the exercises does not matter very much. It is best to use different muscles in turn, so that a leg exercise is followed by a trunk exercise and then an arm exercise, and so on.

C1 TO C5

The same as S1 to S5. Do them thoroughly, but go for speed. All can be done on a carpet or mat. For C1, clasp a book behind your neck when doing your sit-ups. This makes it harder.

C6   BENCH STEPPING

Stand in front of the bench or chair, and step up onto it with the right leg. Bring the other leg up so that you are for a brief moment standing straight up on the bench, then step down again. Do this thirty to fifty times.

C7   PULL-UPS

Hang by your arms from a beam or the top of the stairs. Pull your body up until your chin comes up to the level of your hands. Repeat three to eight times.

C8   ALTERNATE PRESS

Holding a brick, heavy stone or weight in each hand, push each hand alternately up toward the ceiling. Do twenty to forty times.

C9   CURLS

Pick up a pile of two or three bricks, with both hands underneath them. Standing with feet apart, curl your arms up toward your chest and then back again. Do this ten to twenty times.

C10   HEART-TRAINING EXERCISE

Skipping or running on the spot, for three to five minutes; start at a steady pace. When you reach the last minute, put in thirty seconds of intense effort, then finish up with thirty seconds at the original pace.

WEIGHT TRAINING AT HOME

Weight training is normally done under supervision in a properly equipped gym. For the keep-fit enthusiast who wants to keep up his all-around strength without a great deal of time and expense, the following set of exercises will suffice. They should be done twice a week, and may be counted as a Level B form of exercise. Because they do not count as heart-training exercises, you will still have to fit in three sessions of heart training a week to consider yourself really fit.

EQUIPMENT

Because I am recommending the use of light weights only, you need not spend very much. You will need an iron bar, five or six feet long, with four clips or fasteners to prevent the weights from sliding about. You will need two 5-pound weights, two 10-pound weights and two 20-pound weights. If you count the weight of the bar and fasteners as 10 pounds, this will give you the capability of loads varying from 10 to 80 pounds.

PROGRESSION

For each exercise, start with a load that you can handle easily. Make sure that you are lifting it properly before you go up to heavier weights. When you can repeat the exercise *ten times fast*, it is time to move up to a heavier weight. When you move up to a higher weight, be satisfied with doing the exercise five or six times slowly and increase the number of repetitions and the speed in later weeks.

It is important that you not try to increase the load too quickly; if you do, you will not get the desired training effect. This set of exercises, done with light weights and large numbers of fast repetitions, will not produce great strength or bulging muscles, but it will produce fit muscles, with a combination of strength and endurance.

WEIGHT-TRAINING SCHEDULE

Start with one set of flexibility and strength exercises, then go three times through the set of five weight exercises. Start with six repetitions at the lowest poundage shown, then move up in number of repetitions.

W1 CURLS (STOMACH AND BACK)

Start at 30 pounds. Stand with feet apart, holding the bar with palms uppermost, arms hanging down. Keeping your back straight, curl your arms upward so as to bring the bar up to your chest. Lower slowly to original position. Try to breathe normally throughout.

W2 BENCH PRESS (ARMS AND SHOULDERS)

Start at 40 pounds. Lie on your back, feet together, with the bar across your chest and your hands under the bar. Straighten your arms, pushing the bar upward; then lower it again until it is just above your chest.

W3 OVERHEAD PRESS (UPPER BODY)

Start at 40 pounds. Squat in front of the bar, with your back straight and your head up. Place your hands on the bar, just wider apart than your shoulders. Straighten your knees and, keeping your back straight, lift the bar so that it is level with your collarbone. This should be done in one swift and continuous movement. Now push the bar upward until your arms are straight, and lower it again to your collarbone. At the end of the exercise lower the bar gently to the ground, *still keeping your back straight.*

W4 STEP-UPS (CALVES AND ANKLES)

Start at 40 pounds. The bar should be resting across the back of your neck, held but not supported by your arms. A rolled-up towel or shirt under the bar will prevent it from pressing too hard on your backbone. Step onto a firm bench or chair, about twenty inches high, straightening your knees as the back leg comes up onto the bench; then step down again. Do fifteen to thirty of these.

W5 HALF-SQUATS (THIGHS)

Start at 40 pounds. With the bar across your shoulders as in W4,

179

and your heels raised an inch or two off floor level, for example by the edge of a mat, bend your knees until you are halfway down to a full squatting position, then straighten up again. In the half-squat position your thighs are at right angles with your shins. Do this twelve to twenty times.

USE OF EXERCISE MACHINES AND OTHER APPARATUS

The advantage of using rowing machines or static bicycles for exercise is that they can be used at any time of the day or night, and at any time of year. They should therefore make it easier for you to keep up to the mark. Furthermore, a good machine will afford some means of calibrating the work load, so that if you also measure the time spent on the machine, you know exactly what you have done and can measure your progress. You can gradually build up the load so as to get a heart-training effect, or you can work for a longer time with a lighter load and get an endurance benefit.

The disadvantages are that the machines cost money and that using them can become extremely boring. However, if they get anyone to take exercise indoors who would otherwise be embarrassed or afraid to take it out of doors, then the money is well spent. Both the rowing-machine type and the static bicycle, if it has a variable braking load, provide effective all-around training and use up plenty of calories, with the rowing machine being slightly the better because it exercises more muscle groups. Neither is very good for flexibility, and they tend to be used for too short a time to build endurance.

Much less useful for the "keep-fit" man are the muscle-building machines that utilize springs. The general effect is the same as using weights, in that they can be employed to build up the strength of certain muscle groups. They might be useful as an adjunct to training, where someone needs to develop, say, stronger back muscles or biceps. They do not build all-around fitness, because they do nothing for the heart and lungs, nothing for flexibility or endurance, and they do not use up many calories. They might make you look a little better.

Isometric strength training has received a lot of publicity in recent years. It has the great advantage of needing no apparatus. It does serve to increase muscle strength, though not muscle endurance, and so can be used in a training plan, along with other forms of training. It is not the complete training system that some would claim, and in my opinion the use of weights is more satisfying, in that it demonstrates your progress.

APPENDIX

CALORIE CONSUMPTION

Food	Calories per ounce	Food	Calories per ounce
Apples, fresh	13	Ham, cooked	123
Bacon	115	Jam and marmalade	74
Banana	22	Lamb, rib chop	118
Beans, baked	26	Lentils	84
Beef, corned	66	Milk, condensed	100
fresh	91	evaporated	44
Bread	69	whole	19
Buns	84	Onions	7
Butter and margarine	226	Orange	10
Cabbage	7	Peach, canned	19
Caramel candy	118	Peas	18
Cheese, cheddar	120	Pork	119
Chicken	39	Potato	25
Chocolate, plain	155	Potato chips	68
Cookies	158	Prunes	46
Cooking fat	262	Rice	102
Cornflakes	100	Sausage, pork	97
Crackers	123	Sugar	112
Eggs, fresh	46	Syrup and honey	83
Fish, fried	58	Tea and coffee	0
Flour	99	Vegetables, average	5

ENERGY EXPENDITURE

Exercise	Calories per hour (for 140-pound man)
Basal metabolism (additional to all activities)	75
Cycling	175
Dancing	300
Football, soccer	300–550
Gardening	300
Heavy work	400–500
Housework, light	100
heavy	225
Lab work	70
Office work	50
Running	500–900
Sitting	30
Sleep	0
Standing	40
Walking	140
Washing	70

BIBLIOGRAPHY

Chapter 1
"The Kung Bushmen of the Kalahari," R. B. Lee; "Blood Pressures of Kung Bushmen in Northern Botswana," Truswell, Kennelly, Hansen and Lee; "Studies among the Eastern Hadza," J. Woodburn, and "The Life of the Ainu," Hitoshi Watanabe, from *Man the Hunter*, ed. Richard B. Lee and Irven DeVore (Aldine, 1966). 1966).

"Blood Pressure in Bushmen of the Kalahari Desert," *Circulation*, 22, 289, 1960.

African Ecology and Human Evolution, Clark and Bauliere (Methuen, 1964).

Man Adapting, René Dubos (Yale University, 1965).

Chapter 2
"Blood Pressure and Body Build in an African Tribe Living on a Diet of Meat and Milk," Shaper, Williams and Spencer, *E. Afr. Med. J.*, 38, 569, 1961.

"Cardiovascular Disease in the Masai," Mann, Shaffer, Anderson and Sanderstead, *J. Atherosclerosis Res.*, 4, 289, 1964.

"Race and Blood Pressure," R. R. H. Lovell, from *Epidemiology of Hypertension*, ed. Stamler, Stamler and Pullman (Grune & Stratton, 1967).

Biology and the Social Crisis, J. K. Brierly (Heinemann, 1967).

"Quantitative Effects of Dietary Fat on Serum Cholesterol in Man," *Amer. J. Clin. Nutr.*, 87, 52, 1965.

"Coronary Risk Factors in Northern India," Wysham,

184

BIBLIOGRAPHY

Kohli and Mulholland, *Amer. Heart J.*, 79, 181, 1970.

"The Peaks of Old Age," Dr. Alexander Leaf, *Observer Magazine*, September 1973.

Chapter 3

Man, Nature and Disease, Richard Fiennes (Weidenfeld & Nicolson, 1964).

Registrar General Statistical Review, 1974 (HMSO).

Avoidable Death, J. Mansfield (Cassell, 1970).

Human Biology, Harrison et al. (OUP, 1964).

The Process of Ageing, Alex Comfort (Weidenfeld & Nicolson, 1965).

This Slimming Business, J. Yudkin (MacGibbon & Kee, 1958).

Overweight: Causes, Cost and Control (Prentice-Hall, 1968).

Experimental Cardiovascular Disease, Hans Selye (Springer, 1970).

Smoking and Health, a report of the Royal College of Physicians (Pitman, 1962).

"Dietary Fat and Sugar," J. Yudkin, *Lancet*, 2, 4, 1964.

"Psychophysiologic Aspects of Cardiovascular Disease," *Science*, 142, 601.

"Diet and Life Span," Silberberg and Silberberg, *Physiol. Rev.*, 35, 342, 1962.

"Coronary Disease and Physical Activity or Work," J. N. Morris, *Brit. Med. J.*, 2, 14–85, 1958.

Chapter 4

Body Time, Gay Gaer Luce (Maurice Temple Smith, 1972).

A Million Years of Man, R. Carrington (Weidenfeld & Nicolson, 1963).

"The Genetics of Human Populations," L. L. Cavalli-Sforza, *Scientific American*, September 1974.

Chapters 6 and 7

Physiology of Exercise, Herbert A. de Vries (Staples Press, 1967).

185

BIBLIOGRAPHY

Energy, Work and Leisure, J. V. G. A. Durnin and R. Passmore (Heinemann, 1967).

Chapter 8
The New Aerobics, Kenneth H. Cooper (Bantam, 1970).
Jogging, W. J. Bowerman and W. E. Harris (Grosset & Dunlap, 1967).

Chapters 9 and 10
Tulloh on Running, M. B. S. Tulloh (Heinemann, 1968).

Chapter 11
Circuit Training, R. E. Morgan and G. T. Adamson (Bell, 1957).

INDEX

[*Italic* page numbers indicate illustrations.]

INDEX

Khayyam, Omar, 76
Kidney disease, 13
Kikuyu (East Africa), 71
Kipling, Rudyard, 53
Knee exercise, 160
Knee injuries, 153
Kung bushmen, 19
 diseases among, 12
 health of, 13–14
 as hunters and gatherers, 11
Kwakiutl tribe, 12
Kwashiorkor, 12

Leakey, Richard, 57
Leg exercises, 159, 165–67, 171
Lewis, Larry, 82
Life expectancy, 13, 43
Life-styles, diversity of, 73
Ligament strains, 153
Longevity, 31–32
 See also Life expectancy
Lung cancer
 in primitive societies, 14
 and smoking, 93
Lungs, and breathing, 92

Magic, in tribal religion, 21
Malaysian jungle dwellers, 14
Malnutrition, 16, 28
Man
 biological history of, 57
 and ecosystem, 15
 See also Primitive man
Marathon running, 107, 149
Masai tribe (East Africa), 22–23, 24, 25, 26, 38, 53
Meat, vs. vegetables, 10–12
Medical advances, and life expectancy, 43
Medical checkup, before exercise, 97–98
Medicines, in U.S. households, 45
Men
 average body weight, 98–99
 running test for, 104
Mesomorphic body type, 98
Mesopotamian city dwellers, 42
Metabolic rate, and thyroid gland, 86
Micronesian islanders, 46
Morris, Dr. J. N., 47

Mountain villages, longevity in, 31–32
Muscle pulls, 152–53
Muscles
 and circulation, 52
 and exercise machines, 180–81
 overuse of, 63–64
 and posture, 79, 84
 strains, 84, 149
 and weight training, 178
Muscular endurance, 81–83, 100
Muscular strength, 79–81, 100

Natural selection, and climate, 57–58
Neanderthal Man, 59
Neck exercise, 155
Nile basin city dwellers, 42
Nonathletes, fitness for, 108
Nootka tribe, 12
North American Indians, 11
Nunamiut tribe, 12
Nutritional deficiencies, 48

Old age, and community involvement, 32
Ostbye, Eric, 83
Overcrowding, 30, 69
 and life expectancy, 31
Overeating
 and body weight, 48–50
 before exercise, 153
Overload response, of body, 64
Oxygen intake, see Heart fitness

Paleolithic hunters, 19
Parasites, and primitive man, 14–15
Pastoral nomads, 22–28
Pepsin (enzyme), 10
Performance, and body rhythms, 65
Personality, 72
 and family responsibility, 71
Plague, and life expectancy, 43
Plains Indians (America), 22, 25
Pneumonia, deaths from, in U.S., 45
Polarization, and overcrowding, 69
Poliomyelitis, death rates for, 43
Population
 control, 16, 25
 world, 68–69

INDEX

Posture
  and muscles, 79, 84
  and running, 149–50
Press
  alternate, *41*, 177
  bench, 179
  overhead, 179
Primitive man
  and accidents, 15
  blood pressure of, 13, 24
  culture system of, 19–21
  diet of, 10–12, 17
  and diseases, 13–15
  mating instinct of, 18
Primitive societies
  birth control in, 16
  muscular endurance in, 82
  role playing in, 71–72
Protein
  deficiency, 30–31
  intake, 11
Proust, Marcel, 76
Puerto Rico, death rates from heart
    disease in, 46
Pugh, Dr. Griffiths, 112
Pull-ups, 177
Pulse rate, counting, 101–102
Purpose, in life, 75–77
Push-ups, 174
Pygmy tribe (Central Africa), 14, 18
Pyke, Magnus, 51

Rarajipari (kick-ball game), 29, 37
Repetition running, 117
Resistance running, 117
Rewards, and culture system, 20
Rhythms, body, 64–66
Rickets, 12
Ritual, in tribal religion, 20–21
Roads, running on, 150–51, 152
Role playing
  and culture system, 20
  and family, 70
Rome, city life in, 42
Roughage, in diet, 48
Rowing machines, 180
Rubaiyat (Omar Khayyam), 76
Running, 61–62, 103–104, 116–17
  clothing for, 147–48
  footwear for, 148–49
  injuries from, 151–53

places for, 150–51
posture and, 149–50
warming up, 149
  See also Marathon running
Rustam (young Asian), 66–67

Sahara hunter-gatherers, 12
Salt, and blood pressure, 13
Samburu tribe (East Africa), 23, 24,
    38, 46
Selye, Dr. Hans, 94
Sex, as exercise, 95
"Shin splints," 151
Shoes, for running, 148–49, 152, 153
Shoulder exercises, 156–57, 162–63,
    179
Side exercise, 161
Sit-ups, 169–70
Ski orienteering, 114
Smoking, 32
  and diseases, 47, 93
South Africa, heart disease in, 46
Spartan systems, and tribal instinct,
    54
Speed, and muscular strength, 80
Spine exercises, 165–67
Splints, 152
Sports, 112–14
  and culture system, 29–30
  and energy use, 89–90
Step-ups, 179
Stewart, Jackie, 113
Stiffness, 152
  and exercise, 84–85
  and muscle use, 63
Stitch, 153
Stomach exercise, 179
Strapping, and muscle pulls, 152–53
Strength exercises, 169–75
Stress
  and blood pressure, 52–54
  tolerance, 94–95
Strokes, 13
  See also Cerebrovascular disease
Subsistence farming, 26–30
Sugar
  and calories, 48
  and dental decay, 51

Tarahumara tribe (Mexico), 28–30,
    36, 37

Tennis, and energy use, 89–90
Tension, see Stress
Thigh exercises, 164, 179–80
Thyroid gland, 86
Tribes
  and family, 75
  and religion, 20–21
  and values, 73–74
  See also Primitive man
Trunk exercises, 158, 161, 162–63
Tuberculosis, death rates for, 43
Turkana tribe, 25

United States
  blood pressure of males, 24
  causes of death in, 43, 45
  exercise programs in, 116
  hypertension in, 13, 46
  life expectancy in, 43
  nutritional deficiencies in, 48
Upper-body exercises, 179

Valium (tranquilizer), 45
Values, and tribes, 73–74

Vegetables, vs. meat, 10–12
Vilcabamba (Andean villagers), 31
Violence, 75
Vitamin-B deficiency, 12
Voltaire, François Marie Arouet de,
  76

Warfare (intertribal), and population
  control, 25
Warrior cult (East Africa), 25
Weight, see Body weight
Weight training
  equipment, 178
  exercises, 179–80
Weston, Edward Payson, 82
Wisdom, and aged people, 20
Women
  average body weight, 99
  and marathon running, 107
  running test for, 104
Wounds, infection of, 15

Yoga, 94, 116

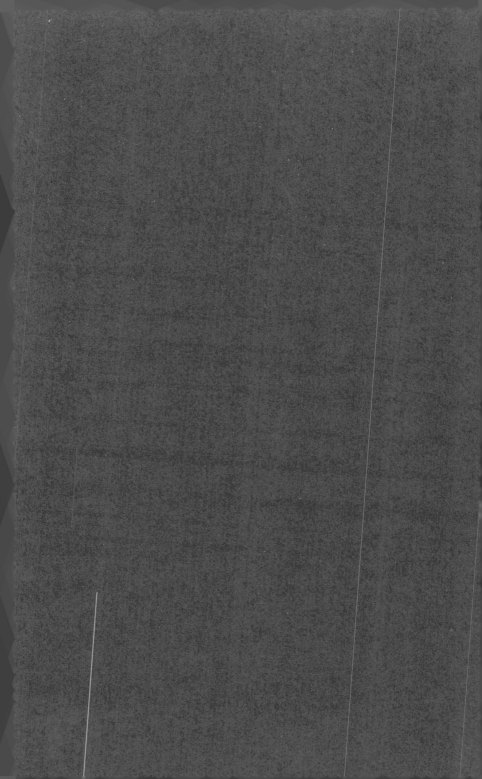